U.S. FORCE STRUCTURE IN NATO

Studies in Defense Policy
TITLES PUBLISHED

Naval Force Levels and Modernization: An Analysis of Shipbuilding Requirements
Arnold M. Kuzmack

Support Costs in the Defense Budget: The Submerged One-Third
Martin Binkin

The Changing Soviet Navy
Barry M. Blechman

Strategic Forces: Issues for the Mid-Seventies
Alton H. Quanbeck and Barry M. Blechman

U.S. Reserve Forces: The Problem of the Weekend Warrior
Martin Binkin

U.S. Force Structure in NATO: An Alternative
Richard D. Lawrence and Jeffrey Record

RICHARD D. LAWRENCE *and* JEFFREY RECORD

U.S. FORCE STRUCTURE IN NATO

An Alternative

A Staff Paper

THE BROOKINGS INSTITUTION
Washington, D.C.

1775 Massachusetts Avenue, N.W., Washington, D.C. 20036

Library of Congress Cataloging in Publication Data:
Lawrence, Richard D 1930–
U.S. force structure in NATO.
(Studies in defense policy)
Includes bibliographical references.
1. North Atlantic Treaty Organization—United States. 2. United States—Military policy. 3. Europe—Defenses. I. Record, Jeffrey, joint author. II. Title. III. Series.
UA646.5.U5L38 355.03'3073 74-1436
ISBN 0-8157-5171-0

9 8 7 6 5 4 3 2 1

THE BROOKINGS INSTITUTION is an independent organization devoted to nonpartisan research, education, and publication in economics, government, foreign policy, and the social sciences generally. Its principal purposes are to aid in the development of sound public policies and to promote public understanding of issues of national importance.

The Institution was founded on December 8, 1927, to merge the activities of the Institute for Government Research, founded in 1916, the Institute of Economics, founded in 1922, and the Robert Brookings Graduate School of Economics and Government, founded in 1924.

The Board of Trustees is responsible for the general administration of the Institution, while the immediate direction of the policies, program, and staff is vested in the President, assisted by an advisory committee of the officers and staff. The by-laws of the Institution state, "It is the function of the Trustees to make possible the conduct of scientific research, and publication, under the most favorable conditions, and to safeguard the independence of the research staff in the pursuit of their studies and in the publication of the results of such studies. It is not a part of their function to determine, control, or influence the conduct of particular investigations or the conclusions reached."

The President bears final responsibility for the decision to publish a manuscript as a Brookings book or staff paper. In reaching his judgment on the competence, accuracy, and objectivity of each study, the President is advised by the director of the appropriate research program and weighs the views of a panel of expert outside readers who report to him in confidence on the quality of the work. Publication of a work signifies that it is deemed to be a competent treatment worthy of public consideration; such publication does not imply endorsement of conclusions or recommendations contained in the study.

The Institution maintains its position of neutrality on issues of public policy in order to safeguard the intellectual freedom of the staff. Hence interpretations or conclusions in Brookings publications should be understood to be solely those of the author or authors and should not be attributed to the Institution, to its trustees, officers, or other staff members, or to the organizations that support its research.

FOREWORD

American forces in Europe have long been a subject of debate in the United States. The debate, as it concerns the likelihood of conflict, the political purposes served by the U.S. military presence, and the equitable sharing of its costs, was treated in a 1971 Brookings book, *U.S. Troops in Europe: Issues, Costs, and Choices,* by John Newhouse with Melvin Croan, Edward R. Fried, and Timothy W. Stanley. More recently, as reflected in various administration and other proposals, a related question has received public attention: whether the military structure of U.S. NATO forces is properly adapted to the threat posed by the Soviet Union and its Warsaw Pact allies.

In this staff paper, Richard D. Lawrence and Jeffrey Record suggest that the present U.S. military posture on the European continent is dangerously inappropriate. Their assessment of Soviet forces reveals a military establishment designed almost exclusively for a short, intense war characterized by massive offensive operations; in contrast, American forces are deployed largely for protracted conflict. The authors call for major changes in the organization and disposition of U.S. forces—whether abroad or at home—available for combat in Europe. They believe that their proposed changes can prepare American forces in Europe for effective defense in a short war and can lead to costs and manpower levels lower than those now associated with the European deployment, without increasing current force levels or military budgets of the U.S. defense establishment as a whole.

The presumption of a short, intense war as the most likely threat in Europe has recently received official recognition in Secretary of Defense James R. Schlesinger's *Annual Defense Department Report, Fiscal Year 1975*. The authors' prescriptions for restructuring U.S. forces available for European contingencies are similar in broad outline, though not in detail, to those offered by Secretary Schlesinger.

Colonel Richard D. Lawrence, now the commanding officer of the First Brigade of the First Cavalry Division at Fort Hood, Texas, was a Federal Executive Fellow at the Brookings Institution in 1972–73. Jeffrey Record is a research associate and Rockefeller Younger Scholar on the defense analysis staff of the Brookings Foreign Policy Studies program, which is directed by Henry Owen.

The Brookings Institution thanks the members of its Defense Analysis Advisory Board—Philip Odeen, George H. Quester, Stanley M. Resor, Charles Rossotti, Henry S. Rowen, and R. James Woolsey—for their helpful comments on this paper. Others who gave generously of their time to comment on the manuscript include Philip J. Farley, Major General Rolland V. Heiser, Lieutenant General James G. Kalergis, Robert W. Komer, Major General George C. Loving, Jr., and Rear Admiral Harry D. Train II. The authors are grateful for the suggestions of their Brookings colleagues Barry M. Blechman, Edward R. Fried, Alton H. Quanbeck, Henry Owen, and William D. White; to Virginia C. Haaga, who edited the manuscript; and to Louisa Thoron, who checked the data and references.

The Institution also acknowledges the assistance of the Ford Foundation, whose grant helps to support its defense and foreign policy studies. The views expressed here are those of the authors and should not be ascribed to the Ford Foundation or to the trustees, officers, or other staff members of the Brookings Institution.

KERMIT GORDON
President

May 1974
Washington, D.C.

CONTENTS

Appendixes

Tables

Figures

GLOSSARY

AFCENT Allied Forces Central Europe

AFNORTH Allied Forces North

Benelux Belgium, the Netherlands, and Luxembourg

CENTAG Central Army Group

Central Region West Germany (minus Schleswig-Holstein), the Benelux countries, East Germany, Poland, and Czechoslovakia

CONUS Continental United States

D day The day on which hostilities begin

DDR East Germany

Division Force A U.S. Army division, its Initial Supporting Increment, and its Sustaining Supporting Increment

FGR Federal Republic of Germany (West Germany)

GSFG Group of Soviet Forces in [East] Germany

ISI Initial Supporting Increment

LOC Line of communication

MBFR Mutual and balanced force reductions

M day The day on which mobilization begins

MLC Multinational logistics command

NATO North Atlantic Treaty Organization

NATO Center West Germany minus Schleswig-Holstein

NORTHAG Northern Army Group

RCD Reserve Cadre Division

SACEUR Supreme Allied Commander, Europe

SSI Sustaining Supporting Increment

USAREUR U.S. Army, Europe

USAF United States Air Force

USAFE U.S. Air Forces in Europe

CHAPTER ONE

INTRODUCTION

The global structure of power is today in a state of marked transition. Politically a bipolar world has given way to a multipolar one, and the traditional post–World War II economic order is undergoing radical readjustment. East and West will have to adjust to these unsettling changes, as will their respective alliances. NATO, because it is fundamentally an international and not a supranational organization, will perhaps be less able to bear the stress of a changing world order than will the Warsaw Pact,[1] an alliance of enforced rather than voluntary allegiance. Thus it is clear that if the Atlantic Alliance is to maintain its political viability and at the same time provide an effective counter to Soviet military power in Europe, a review of its purpose and a careful assessment of the means of achieving that purpose in light of changing conditions are in order.

A major issue confronting NATO, upon which the unity of the alliance could easily founder, is the future of U.S. military power in Europe. The continued presence in Europe of over three hundred thousand American troops has become a topic of growing and often heated controversy in recent years. Expanding congressional pressures for reducing their number reflect the American public's general post-Vietnam discontent with large and ongoing U.S. military commitments abroad and its specific and more pronounced resentment of what is perceived to be a refusal on the part of a prosperous and powerful Western Europe to bear its fair share of NATO defense burdens. This sentiment is exacerbated by rising irritation with European economic competition and by

1. The Warsaw Pact is a multilateral military alliance formed under Soviet direction in 1955. The present members of the alliance are the USSR, Poland, East Germany, Czechoslovakia, Hungary, Rumania, and Bulgaria.

what is perceived as a seemingly endless drain by U.S. troops and their dependents on the U.S. balance of payments.

Moreover, the feeling of expanding Soviet-American détente has served to undercut in the public mind the need for U.S. troops in Europe. Indeed, the discussions of mutual and balanced force reductions (MBFR) now under way in Vienna are not only testimony to the erosion of the very cold war tensions that led to the stationing of those troops on the continent, but also an indication that a significant military stand-down in Europe may well be negotiated before the end of the seventies.

Pressures and opportunities for change are thus great and growing. The principal question addressed in this study is whether, without considerable change in the framework of existing active forces both at home and abroad, an alternative U.S. conventional force posture in NATO can be devised that would be more attuned to the real threat—short war—and at the same time somewhat less costly in men and money than the present posture. The primary objective is to investigate new organizations and dispositions to accomplish those aims. The authors believe that the adoption of at least the principles underlying most of their proposals would improve the effectiveness of U.S. forces in Europe as long as they remained on the continent in sizable numbers.

This of course does not rule out the prospect of developing different force postures by other means, including radical cuts in active U.S. force levels, though such measures go beyond the intended scope of this study since they would require fundamental changes in the basic criteria for defense planning.

The proposals made here are based on a number of assumptions:

- *The security of Western Europe is vital to the United States.* The authors believe that the safety and well-being of Western Europe and America are inextricably interdependent.

- *The need to balance Soviet military power in Central Europe continues.* Admittedly the prospects of a Soviet-initiated war on the continent are probably more remote now than at any time since the end of the Second World War. Yet conflict stemming from accident or miscalculation cannot be ruled out. Moreover, as is shown in the authors' own assessment of Soviet force posture and military doctrine, there persists a disquieting contradiction between the official rationale for Russian forces west of the Urals and their size, disposition, and structure. In any event, maintenance of a perceived balance is essential to détente, to Western cooperation in the economic field, and to the continued dominance of moderate political forces in the Federal Republic of Germany.

• *U.S. membership in NATO is essential to the maintenance of an effective balance of military power in Central Europe.* America's contribution to the Atlantic Alliance represents the core of NATO's ability both to deter and to counter aggression. Stripped of a reliable U.S. nuclear guarantee and of adequate U.S. conventional forces, Europe probably would not be able to muster the forces needed to counter existing Soviet military strength in Eastern Europe and the western USSR.

• *The objectives of deterrence and détente are valid and mutually compatible.* The authors recognize the potential inconsistencies between the two; however, they believe that successful détente depends upon NATO's retaining a credible defense at each stage of East-West negotiations.

• *A forward nonnuclear defense of Western Europe is not only feasible but also well within the capability of the conventional forces that are currently available to NATO.* The gloom that has traditionally pervaded discussions of conventional defense within military circles of both NATO and some of its member states is not shared by the authors. They feel that this pessimism results from exaggerations of the Soviet threat and, in some cases, of a refusal to contemplate any response to invasion other than an almost instantaneous nuclear riposte.

The authors' appraisal of the military balance suggests that whatever the weaknesses of NATO, they are not for the most part attributable to an insufficiency of forces. Similarly the deepening congressional debate over the size of U.S. forces committed to Europe has so far skirted what the authors feel are equally important issues—the location of U.S. forces and their readiness, structure, and mission orientation.

The study begins with what the authors believe is a realistic appraisal of the Warsaw Pact threat in NATO's Central Region, followed by an assessment of the present U.S. contribution to the region's conventional defense. Particular attention is paid to those aspects of the respective force postures of the United States and NATO and of the Warsaw Pact that indicate the kind of war for which both sides have prepared and which they are most capable of waging.

Next a summary of the weaknesses of NATO's, and especially the United States', force posture vis-à-vis that of the Pact forms the basis for constructing an alternative force posture designed to overcome those weaknesses and for estimating the savings in manpower and funds that might be achieved. The final chapter places specific alternatives in perspective and discusses how changes in force posture might be made so as to meet allied concerns.

The military environment on which the study focuses is that of conventional war—the level of conflict that U.S. general purpose forces are primarily designed to deter and if necessary to fight. Though the implications of tactical nuclear deployments in Europe are discussed, they are not the focal point of the study. The primary focus of the book is on ground forces, which are the core of U.S. combat power in Europe. While a detailed investigation of issues related to tactical air posture is beyond the scope of the study, the authors do try to identify the broader implications for U.S. tactical air forces of a short-war ground force posture. Naval forces are not considered here since their contribution to ground combat in the Central Region is relatively marginal and because questions of naval force structure in Europe hinge upon worldwide sea power considerations.

Marked emphasis is placed on the Central Region—the West German border from Lauenburg to Passau—because it clearly would be the major arena of East-West military confrontation in Europe. While NATO's northern and southern flanks are important, they are of peripheral concern to this study, since both NATO and the Pact have deployed the bulk of their combat-ready ground forces in the Central Region. Furthermore, the region's proximity to key military, economic, and political targets in Western Europe makes it the decisive sector in any major war on the continent.

Finally, since so much of the discussion that follows involves an assessment of the military requirements for a short as opposed to a protracted war, it is necessary at the outset to define them both. The authors' conception of a short war in the European context (based on their analyses of the structure of Soviet forces and doctrine and on the presumption that the Pact initiates the hostilities) is one that would last no longer than two or at most three months and would be characterized by intensive combat and high rates of attrition. This is not to suggest that fighting would terminate abruptly after that period but rather that the ultimate outcome of the contest—barring a major escalation by either side—should be fairly apparent by then. More specifically, within this time, it should become clear whether a Pact offensive against NATO Center will succeed or be halted and contained by NATO forces. However, reinforcements and resupply activity on both sides might continue for a longer period as each force tried to maintain tactical stability in the war zone and deny its opponent an opportunity to renew its strategy successfully. Such activity could perhaps continue even as negotiations were begun. By protracted war the authors mean one lasting many months or even several years.

CHAPTER TWO

THE THREAT: THE WARSAW PACT AND SHORT WAR

U.S. and NATO forces are designed to balance communist military power in Eastern Europe and in the western Soviet Union. That power is represented by the Warsaw Pact. An assessment of the Pact's military organization, intentions, doctrines, and capabilities—the purpose of this chapter—is essentially an analysis of Soviet military dispositions. Not only is the USSR the sole nuclear member of the alliance and thus the exclusive repository of the Pact's strategic deterrent, it also supplies the bulk of the Pact's conventional forces. Not surprisingly it dominates virtually all of the Pact's decision-making processes.

Intentions

Threat is a combination of intentions and capabilities. As a creature of Soviet aims and power in Europe, the Warsaw Pact harbors no intentions separable from those of the Soviet Union. Although Russia's ultimate political objectives in Western Europe remain a subject of considerable controversy in the West, the Soviets so far have refrained from using force against NATO to achieve them. As has already been noted, the chance of a Soviet-initiated armed conflict in Europe is remote. Yet the possibility of some future limited military action taken to influence the outcome of a diplomatic crisis is a legitimate concern for NATO, as is the prospect of hostilities spawned by accident or miscalculation. Moreover, the political implications of a widely perceived imbalance between Pact and NATO military power could be enormous—in checking *Ostpolitik* and incipient Soviet-American détente, as well as in creating new problems in intra-European community and transatlantic relations.

From a purely military standpoint, however, the greatest source of Western anxiety is perhaps the disparity between the stated rationale for Soviet forces in Europe and their actual posture. In truth it has been more the *character* and less the fact of Russian military power on the continent that has generated the most uneasiness among specialists in the West since the end of World War II. The sheer mass of the Soviet presence in Eastern Europe exceeds any conceivable requirement either for the preservation of Soviet political preponderance there or for the successful defense of the Pact from NATO forces, which, as currently postured, are incapable of sustaining a strategic offensive.[1] Analysis in this chapter will show that the disposition, structure, readiness, and tactical doctrine of Soviet forces deployed west of the Russian border suggest deliberate preparation of offensive, rather than defensive, military operations.

Of further interest is the fact that the USSR's growing extra-European military needs have not been met at the expense of its forces in Eastern Europe or in the Mediterranean. On the contrary, since the mid-1960s, in spite of Russia's formidable military buildup along the Sino-Soviet border and its notable projection of surface naval power beyond European waters, the number of Soviet divisions in Eastern Europe has actually *increased* (as a result of the occupation of Czechoslovakia in 1968), as has the size of Russia's permanent naval presence in the Mediterranean.

Command and Organizational Structure

That the Pact is largely an instrument, if not a mere extension, of Soviet military power in Europe is nowhere more obvious than in its command and organizational structure, which has been tightly controlled by the USSR since the alliance began under Moscow's sponsorship in 1955. Ostensibly a collective security organization designed to counter

1. There is, of course, a direct but indeterminate link between Soviet garrisons and the USSR's political leverage in Eastern Europe. From a purely military standpoint, however, it is questionable whether even a token presence is necessary to ensure Moscow's ability to intervene forcibly in the affairs of individual Pact states. For example, the lack of a Soviet military presence in Czechoslovakia in 1968 did not prevent a lightning occupation of that country by the USSR and replacement of its "deviant" regime. Conversely the presence of Soviet forces has actually contributed to violent anti-Russian uprisings: the revolts in East Germany in 1953 and in Hungary three years later are but two examples.

a NATO bolstered by West German membership, the Pact has served to legitimize the Soviet military presence in Eastern Europe and provide a facade for Russian intervention.

The Pact is formally organized around a Political Consultative Committee and a Joint High Command, both of which are located in Moscow. Normally composed of the foreign ministers of the member states, and always chaired by the appropriate Soviet representative, the committee is a forum for generating common military and political policies vis-à-vis the West. Assisting the committee is a Joint Secretariat and a Permanent Commission, both headed by Soviet officials.

The Joint High Command, whose purpose according to the 1955 treaty is "to strengthen the defense capability of the Warsaw Pact, to prepare military plans in case of war and to decide on the deployment of troops,"[2] consists of a commander-in-chief, a chief of staff, a Defense Committee, a Military (Main) Staff, and a Military Council. The USSR's domination of the Joint Command is no less complete than its control of the Political Consultative Committee. The key positions of commander-in-chief and of chief of staff have always been filled by senior Soviet officers. The Military Council, which "seems to be the main channel through which the Pact's orders are transmitted to its forces in peacetime,"[3] is headed by the commander-in-chief and composed of the chief of staff and standing military representatives assigned to the council from each of the member states' armed forces. Virtually all of the important planning undertaken by the Military Staff is conducted by Soviet officers. Only the Defense Committee appears to be relatively free from Russian control; its main functions, however, are purely advisory. Established in the wake of the Soviet invasion of Czechoslovakia because of increased pressure on the USSR for a greater Eastern European voice in directing joint military activities, the committee is composed of the defense ministers of the member states.

The precise command relationship between the various national armies and the Soviet General Staff remains a matter of some speculation. Recent developments suggest, however, that substantial progress has been made toward meeting Russia's long-standing goal of an integrated Pact military force under the operational control of the Soviet General Staff. In the 1969 session of the Political Consultative Com-

2. International Institute for Strategic Studies, *The Military Balance 1972–1973* (London: IISS, 1972), p. 10.

3. Ibid.

mittee in Budapest, provisions were made for a more integrated Military Staff, for the appointment of a national deputy to the Russian commander in each country where Soviet units are stationed, and for the creation of a "Co-ordination Body for War Technique," designed to centralize logistics organization and to coordinate the procurement, if not the development, of weapons. These measures were facilitated by the increasing number of joint Soviet-directed peacetime military maneuvers conducted in Eastern Europe and by the almost total dependence of Eastern European military establishments on the USSR for both weapons and logistics support.

Further steps were taken in 1970 when Eastern European military forces underwent a major reorganization in which selected units were formally assigned to positions within the *Soviet* order of battle. Moreover, the air defense system that screens the entire Warsaw Pact region is currently centered in Moscow and is directed by the commander-in-chief of the Soviet Air Defense Forces.

Russian control over the Pact's military apparatus is thus clearly decisive. As one observer has concluded, "for administrative, operational and logistical purposes the Warsaw Pact is being run on the lines of a Soviet Military District and the military forces of the Pact organised as yet another 'arm' of the Soviet armed forces."[4]

Soviet Military Doctrine and Continental Strategy

Of great importance to any assessment of Soviet military power in Europe are the growing indications that Soviet military doctrine has finally accepted the fact that a war on the continent need not be a nuclear one and that, in any event, the primary wartime mission of Russian ground forces continues to be the rapid conquest of Western Europe.

During the Khrushchev era Soviet doctrine denied the possibility of a major conventional war in Europe. Also rejected was the idea that a nuclear conflict on the continent might be preceded by a short conventional war. The period 1953–64 witnessed the gradual erosion of the customary Russian view of ground forces as the decisive element in war and the eventual triumph of a doctrine that heralded the "primacy of nuclear weapons" and gave to conventional forces the secondary role

4. John Erickson, *Soviet Military Power* (London: Royal United Services Institute for Defense Studies, 1971), pp. 103–04.

of mopping up pockets of enemy resistance that might survive the initial nuclear exchange. When the Strategic Rocket Forces were set up as a separate service, along with the Army, Navy, Air Force, and Air Defense Command, there were substantial reductions in the size of the Soviet Army; as the preeminent service, the rocket forces received a major share of budgetary outlays for defense.

Since Khrushchev's fall in October 1964, there have been three major Soviet military developments: (1) the achievement of a rough strategic parity with the United States, (2) "an increasingly obvious effort . . . to break out of the bounds of the continental Eurasian geostrategic shell without relying directly on intercontinental missiles,"[5] and (3) a return to the traditional emphasis on ground forces. Although the Strategic Rocket Forces remain the paramount arm of the Soviet military, ground and tactical air forces have recovered much of their former prominence.

Indeed, current doctrine reflects a distinct retreat from Khrushchev's version of massive retaliation and a notable adjustment to the strategy of flexible response, which was adopted by the United States in the early 1960s and was finally endorsed by NATO in 1967. Admittedly, however, it remains

> the Soviet view that in present circumstances any major hostilities in Central Europe would almost certainly involve the early introduction of tactical nuclear weapons given the existence of large numbers of these weapons in the region and taking into account the frequent statements by Western spokesmen that in such a situation NATO would be forced, because of its inferiority in conventional forces, to resort to a nuclear response within a matter of days.[6]

Yet the chance of a large-scale subnuclear conflict is receiving the increasing attention of the Soviet High Command. Recent Soviet military literature, the USSR's current upgrading of its own as well as Eastern European conventional forces, and the growing number of military exercises conducted in postulated nonnuclear environments suggest that the Russians are preparing for at least a conventional phase of a general war on the continent.

Whatever the environment, however, and regardless of the circumstances attending the outbreak of major hostilities, the principal mission of Soviet ground forces, which are trained and equipped to operate on

5. Andro Gabelic, "New Accent in Strategy," *Military Review*, Vol. 48 (August 1968), p. 84.

6. Trevor Cliffe, *Military Technology and the European Balance*, Adelphi Papers, 89 (London: International Institute for Strategic Studies, 1972), pp. 29–30.

either a nuclear or a nonnuclear battleground, is basically the same: to occupy Western Europe by means of a massive blitzkrieg. That Russia's conventional forces are charged primarily with offensive operations at the theater level not only is confirmed by Soviet military literature, which uniformly contends that the "offensive is the main type of combat actions,"[7] but also is revealed in the size, disposition, and structure of Soviet ground and tactical air forces deployed west of the Urals.

Russian perceptions of continental combat at the conventional level were accurately summarized in a recent study by John Erickson:

> *Mobile operations* and *manoeuvre* are, in the Soviet view, the concomitant of the use of nuclear weapons [or the threat of their use]. The large sectors for deployment are reduced to the narrower attack frontages in order to maximise the conditions for overcoming enemy defenses, after which strong armored forces will be loosed into the rear and the deep rear. The anticipated rate of advance is in the order of 70 miles in a 24-hour period, the emphasis is on high-speed attacks, speedy crossing of river lines, the employment of airborne and helicopter-borne forces ahead of the advance, efficient cross-country movement, fighting with open flanks and striking on by night as well as by day. The basic attack form will be "off the march" (without prior concentration) and the "meeting engagement" . . . the accepted form of action, both of them high-speed manoeuvres. . . .[8]

This argues strongly, as does other available evidence, that the Soviets in the event of a major war in Europe have clearly chosen the option of a general offensive as opposed to simply a territorial defense of Eastern Europe.

The only really questionable element of this doctrine of unconditional attack—and one that is of crucial importance to NATO—is the postulated rate of advance. Many Western analysts suggest that the Soviets presume a rate of advance in the neighborhood of seventy miles a day.[9] This pace, if sustained, would bring the Red Army to the Rhine in less than forty-eight hours and to the Channel ports within a week. That the

7. Major General A. Zyryanov, "APCs in the Offensive," *Soviet Military Review* (April 1973), p. 18.

8. Erickson, *Soviet Military Power,* p. 70.

9. Cliffe (in *Military Technology,* p. 33) states flatly that the Soviets expect their armored forces "to advance at an average rate of 60 miles a day or even considerably more, negotiating river crossings with a minimum of delay and continuing the offensive by night as well as by day." Malcolm Mackintosh concludes that "ground force operations are expected to take place at very high speeds, up to seventy-five miles a day across open country." *Juggernaut: A History of the Soviet Armed Forces* (Macmillan, 1967), p. 306.

possibility of such a pace has gained widespread credence in certain Western European military circles is attributable chiefly to an a priori reluctance if not an outright refusal to entertain the idea that Europe might be defensible without resort to nuclear weapons.

Informed speculation leads one to expect a more modest rate of advance. For one thing, an advance of seventy miles a day would be completely unprecedented in the history of armored conflict in Europe. Advances in excess of thirty to forty miles a day were never sustained by Patton's Third Army, Guderian's XIXth Army Corps and later his redoubtable 2nd Panzer Group, or any sizable Soviet armored formation operating in Europe during the Second World War; and most of these gains were made in the absence of significant resistance, an advantage that the Russians would be denied by NATO.[10]

Moreover, the quality and durability of even the most modern Soviet tanks suggest that, long before reaching the Ruhr, a high percentage of Russian armor would suffer extensive operational failures, which the Red Army's existing maintenance capabilities could probably not overcome. For example, the mean miles between failures (that is, the number of miles a tank can be expected to travel before incurring a major operational breakdown that requires extensive repairs) of the Soviet T-62 medium tank is believed to be in the neighborhood of 100 to 125 miles—or about one-third the distance from the East German border to the English Channel. In contrast, for most NATO tanks, which are the products of superior automotive technology, the figure is somewhere between 150 and 200 miles.

Why the Russians continue to postulate such spectacular gains is not clear. Some observers have suggested that it is simply their desire to intimidate the West. Others contend that it stems from conclusions drawn from their own invasion of Czechoslovakia and from Israel's Sinai campaign in 1967. This may well be true although the lessons from both experiences are of doubtful applicability to a congested Western European environment, in which advancing armor could expect to encounter firm resistance. Perhaps more relevant would be the performance of Israeli armor along the Syrian and Sinai fronts during the Mideast war of 1973; despite the benefit (in most cases) of local air superiority, counterattacking Israeli tank forces failed to achieve notably rapid territorial gains.

10. Jeffrey Record, "Armored Advance Rates: An Historical Inquiry," *Military Review*, Vol. 53 (September 1973).

Soviet Military Capabilities

Capabilities are a mix of the quantity and quality of available forces and the planned manner of their employment. As was noted above, the Warsaw Pact's ultimate intentions toward Western Europe are in some measure unclear to the West. This is not the case, however, with respect to the Pact's military capabilities, which are formidable and growing.

A detailed survey of the Pact's conventional military power—divisions, men, tanks, tactical combat aircraft—and mobilization potential appears in Tables 2-4 and 2-5 and in Table 4-1 (Chapter 4), as well as in Appendix B. Our purpose here is to explore the size, disposition, readiness, and structure of that power as determinants of the nature of the Pact threat. The backbone of the Pact's conventional military power is, of course, the Soviet armed forces. Russia's "contribution" to the alliance can hardly be overstated; Soviet forces deployed west of the Urals (including Eastern Europe) account for approximately 60 percent of the combat-ready divisions, 63 percent of the tanks, 70 percent of the ground troops, and 80 percent of the tactical combat aircraft possessed by the Pact.[11] And, as has been noted, the Soviet General Staff holds unchallenged sway over the formulation of strategy and, at least ostensibly, over the ultimate disposition of most non-Soviet Pact military units. More important is the fact that Soviet forces alone give the Pact its capacity for offensive operations as well as its ability to mobilize and deploy substantial reserves.

Ground Forces

The core of the Soviet Union's military power on the continent is some 400,000 ground troops organized around thirty-one combat-ready divisions stationed in Eastern Europe. (See M + 7 data in Table 2-2.) Another sixty divisions are deployed in the western military districts of the USSR (European Russia). Although only about twelve of the sixty are at full strength, over half of the remaining forty-eight divisions could be mobilized within a month. Of the thirty-one divisions in

11. By comparison, U.S. forces currently deployed in Europe account for about 17 percent of the deployed divisions, 19 percent of the tanks, 10 percent of the soldiers, and 16 percent of the combat aircraft available to NATO (including France).

Eastern Europe, twenty are stationed in East Germany and are known collectively as the Group of Soviet Forces in Germany (GSFG). The concentration of such formidable military power in East Germany (the DDR)—almost two-thirds of Russia's entire Eastern European garrison—suggests not only that the Soviets are concerned with maintaining stability in the DDR but also that the GSFG would be the cutting edge of any major thrust into NATO Center and that the primary axis of advance would be across the North German Plain or through the Fulda Gap.[12] Not only is the terrain in those areas more suitable for swift armored penetration than is the more mountainous terrain farther south, but also Soviet forces stationed in the DDR are closer to such key objectives as the Ruhr and the Channel ports than are Soviet or Pact divisions located elsewhere along the Central Front. Other Soviet military formations in Eastern Europe are two divisions in Poland, four in Hungary, and five in Czechoslovakia.

The structure of Russian forces in Eastern Europe, no less than their inordinate size, is further testimony to the doctrine of intense, swift, offensive operations at the theater level. As was noted above, all Soviet divisions stationed in Eastern Europe are at virtually full strength and are combat ready. The bulk of them are deployed in the DDR, opposite the weakest sectors of NATO's Central Front. More indicative of their offensive posture is their tank-heaviness: sixteen of the thirty-one divisions are tank divisions; the remaining fifteen are motorized rifle divisions that have an unusually large number of tanks. The Soviets' strong emphasis on tanks—which are by their nature offensive weapons—is reflected in the high ratio of tanks to men at the division level. For example, although the number of men in a Soviet armored division (8,400) is less than half that in a U.S. armored division (17,500), the former fields almost as many tanks as does the latter. As is shown in Table 2-1,

12. This is the general consensus among Western military analysts, although some German observers, citing the USSR's reluctance to permit its forces in Hungary to become the subject of MBFR negotiations, believe that the Austrian corridor is a more likely route of invasion. The authors, however, believe that the arguments against the Austrian corridor are compelling. Aside from the political onus the USSR would incur by attacking a neutral country, the difficult alpine terrain in Austria and southern Germany virtually precludes rapid armored advances. Moreover, the distances to important objectives in Western Europe are twice those that GSFG formations would have to travel. Finally, an invasion through Austria would require such massive redeployments of Soviet forces from their existing locations in Eastern Europe and the USSR that NATO would be warned well in advance.

Table 2-1. Comparison of U.S.–Soviet Ratios of Tanks to Men in Armored Divisions and Mechanized Infantry and Motorized Rifle Divisions

Type of division	*Number of tanks*	*Number of men*	*Ratio of tanks to men*
Armored			
U.S.	324	17,500	1:54
Soviet	316	8,400	1:27
Mechanized infantry/motorized rifle			
U.S.	216	16,000	1:74
Soviet	188	10,500	1:56

Sources: Based on data in International Institute for Strategic Studies, *The Military Balance 1972–1973* (London: IISS, 1972), p. vii; and John Erickson, *Soviet Military Power* (London: Royal United Services Institute for Defense Studies, 1971), p. 75.

that disparity also holds true for mechanized infantry/motorized rifle divisions, although to a lesser degree.

More striking evidence of Soviet preparation for a short offensive war is the high ratio of combat to support troops at the division level. It is estimated that about 75 percent of Soviet divisional manpower is allocated to combat functions, whereas only 25 percent is assigned to support units, in sharp contrast to U.S. and Western European divisions. Such an extraordinary combat-to-support ratio clearly favors a short war; a protracted conflict would compel the support-poor Soviet forces to revert increasingly to their traditional reliance on inferior and less manageable civilian transportation and supply resources. Thus from a purely logistical standpoint a war of extended duration would be doubly disadvantageous for the Soviets, because on the battlefield they would be confronting NATO formations whose relatively low combat-to-support ratio (about 1:1) permits sustained engagement for longer periods of time.

Indeed, there is some evidence that even a short war might seriously strain the Red Army's meager logistics infrastructure. For example, Soviet forces, to a much greater extent than those of either the United States or its NATO allies, depend on railroads for transporting men and supplies to the front. A Soviet field army (three to five divisions) usually operates from sixty to ninety-five miles of its own railhead, which serves a number of depots within twenty miles of the front. Each depot supports one or two and sometimes three divisions through a road network; trucks thus provide the link between the depots and the front. As the front advances, rail lines are extended and railheads and depots relocated forward.

At least three weaknesses are apparent in the "railhead" approach to supporting frontline combat formations, which is a legacy of Soviet logistics organization during the Second World War. One is that the mobility of modern armored forces promises to advance the front at a pace much faster than railheads and depots could be extended to support it, particularly if the retreating enemy had destroyed rail facilities in the territory about to be occupied. In other words, railheads and depots simply would not be able to "keep up," thus increasing the burden on road-bound transport, in which the Red Army is notoriously deficient.

A second weakness is that rail lines not only are more vulnerable than roads to interdiction by tactical air and guerrilla forces but also require a longer time to repair. No better example of this greater vulnerability exists than the near paralyzing of the German rail network in the Soviet Union by Russian partisans during the Second World War, in contrast to their less successful attempts to block road-bound traffic.

Finally, the gauge of Soviet railroads is wider than that of Eastern and Western European railroads. This difference complicates and delays the movement of forces from Russia's western military districts into Eastern Europe, a key element in Russia's ability to increase its military power along the Central Front.[13]

These and other deficiencies in Soviet logistics support were amply exposed during the invasion of Czechoslovakia in 1968. Despite the absence of armed resistance, advancing Soviet armor quickly outran its rail-based supply depots, and the number of trucks and other logistics support vehicles was not enough to constitute an adequate substitute. (The ratio of unarmored to armored vehicles in a Soviet tank division is 2:1; in contrast, in Western European armored divisions the ratio is 4:1.) As a result,

> during the first week of the occupation . . . a breakdown of transportation and supply services threatened to paralyze the Soviet armies in Czechoslovakia . . . [and] the situation was saved by . . . [an] airlift which delivered fuel, food, and essential equipment. . . .
>
> Under actual combat conditions . . . [Soviet divisions] would have lacked many essential items after the first 24 hour period.[14]

13. The Germans during the Second World War encountered the same obstacle, but in reverse. Troops and supplies headed for the Eastern Front by rail had to be transferred at the Soviet-Polish border onto Russian trains—the only ones suited to Soviet railroads. The resulting delays were exacerbated when the retreating Russian forces destroyed much of their own rolling stock.

14. Leo Heiman, "Soviet Invasion Weaknesses," *Military Review,* Vol. 49 (August 1969), pp. 42–43.

This assessment of Soviet military capabilities has thus far focused on forces in Eastern Europe. Their size, disposition, and structure reveal a military establishment designed for decisive offensive operations in a short war, at the expense of defensive operations geared to the requirements of protracted conflict. It is this *posture* of attack which, in spite of Soviet statements of contrary intentions, continues to generate uneasiness in the West.

Equally disturbing is the USSR's ability to augment its immediately disposable forces along the Central Front. The additional combat troops and tanks that the USSR alone could bring to bear opposite NATO Center within the first sixty days of mobilization exceed the number that NATO could amass, at least at present. (See Table 4-1 in Chapter 4 below.) Yet the clearly superior mobilization capability of the USSR is not enough to justify the argument that Western Europe is conventionally indefensible.

The early postwar image of hundreds of Russian divisions poised for an invasion of Western Europe continues to linger in the public mind despite its effective demolition by many analysts, most notably Alain C. Enthoven and K. Wayne Smith.[15] Although the USSR's 164-division army is the second largest army in the world,[16] it is important to remember that Soviet divisions are little more than half the size of U.S. and NATO divisions and that only about 65 of them (34 motorized rifle, 24 armored, and 7 airborne) are believed to be combat ready. Of this number, about 53 divisions are deployed in Eastern Europe and along the Sino-Soviet border (including 2 divisions in Outer Mongolia); the remaining 12 are believed to be in European Russia.

Appendix B contains a detailed tabular assessment of three potential Warsaw Pact mobilization scenarios. Table 2-2 shows what the authors believe to be the most likely scenario of a Soviet buildup along the Central Front. It is based on calculations of the required mobilization time for each readiness category of divisions, the distance of each division from the Central Front, and certain assumptions with respect to minimum Soviet military requirements outside the European theater. The Red Army's forty-four divisions in the Far East do not appear in the table since it is the authors' conviction that only in extremely desperate

15. *How Much Is Enough? Shaping the Defense Program 1961–1969* (Harper and Row, 1971).

16. The Soviet Union's two million-man army is surpassed only by China's Peoples Liberation Army of 150 divisions and two and one-half million men.

Table 2-2. Most Likely Scenario of a Soviet Buildup of Ground Forces along the Central Front, M Day to M + 120, by Type of Division, Number of Tanks, and Military Manpower

Force component	*M day*[a]	*M + 7*[b]	*M + 15*[c]	*M + 30*[c]	*M + 60*[c]	*M + 90*[c]	*M + 120*[c]
Divisions							
Motorized rifle	13	15	15	23	34	34	40
Tank	14	16	17	27	28	28	29
Airborne	...	...	5	5	5	5	5
Total	27[d]	31	37	55	67	67	74
Tanks[e] (thousands)	6.9	7.9	8.2	12.9	15.2	15.2	16.7
Military manpower (thousands)							
Total deployed[f]	339	401	453	677	842	842	937
Combat troops[g]	254	292	340	508	632	632	703

Sources: Authors' calculations, based on data in International Institute for Strategic Studies, *The Military Balance 1972–1973* (London: IISS, 1972), pp. 5–8; and T. N. Dupuy and Wendell Blanchard, *The Almanac of World Military Power*, 2d ed. (T. N. Depuy Associates, 1972), pp. 150–51.

a. Defined as the day on which mobilization begins.

b. All Soviet ground forces presently stationed in Eastern Europe.

c. For an explanation of the origin of additional forces appearing after M + 7, see Appendix B.

d. All Soviet divisions stationed in Eastern Europe with the exception of the four in Hungary, which are not considered opposite the Center until M + 7.

e. Includes only medium tanks assigned to divisions because they would probably be the only medium tanks fully manned and available for combat.

f. Deployed combat troops plus deployed support troops.

g. Represents 75 percent of total deployed military manpower.

circumstances would thc USSR transfer its forces opposite the Chinese border to the Central Region. Moreover, if the USSR decided to do so, the pace of transfers to the West could be constrained by the limited capacity of the Trans-Siberian Railroad.

A profile of Red Army divisions by type, location, and degree of readiness may also be found in Appendix B. In terms of readiness, Soviet divisions are divided into three categories. Category I divisions, of which there are about sixty-five, are full strength and are believed to be virtually combat ready. Those that are forward deployed against NATO Center include the twenty divisions of the GSFG, the two armored divisions in Poland, and the five divisions located in Czechoslovakia, for a total of twenty-seven.[17] The four Soviet divisions in Hungary, although

17. The Soviet deployment in Czechoslovakia, known as the Central Group of Forces (CGF), does not appear to be postured primarily for a war along the Central Front. The authors have included these divisions in Soviet M-day forces, however, because they probably would be immediately available in a crisis and could not escape almost instantaneous involvement in hostilities.

"The most significant factor of the Group's deployment is that it is not there, as Soviet commentators once claimed, to strengthen the defense of the country against NATO or West Germany. No Soviet formations are stationed on the West German frontier. All divisions are deployed in central Czechoslovakia within striking distance of the main cities, Prague, Bratislava, Olomouc, Brno and Ostrava, and they effectively divide the country in two, cutting off Bohemia and Moravia from Slovakia. This deployment is clearly designed for purposes of internal secu-

combat ready, are three hundred to four hundred miles from the Central Front, as are some Soviet divisions in Czechoslovakia. The transfer of the Soviet divisions in Hungary to the Central Front would completely strip the Pact's southern tier of a Soviet military presence, a prospect that would be politically as well as militarily unattractive to Moscow.[18]

Category II divisions are less ready for combat.[19] Although they are fully outfitted, much of their equipment is in storage and would probably not be operational in less than two weeks. More important, the active M-day personnel strength of Category II divisions is only about 75 percent, thus making necessary a call-up of reservists to provide the remaining 25 percent. Considered deployable at full readiness by M + 30, the approximately fifty-one Category II divisions (twenty-nine motorized rifle and twenty-two armored) in the Red Army are located as follows: twenty-seven in European Russia, two in central USSR, eleven in southern USSR, and eleven in the Far East.

Category III divisions are essentially skeletal units that require major additions of both men and equipment to bring them up to full strength. There are about forty-eight such divisions (twenty-one in European Russia, sixteen in central and southern USSR, and eleven in the Far East), none of which the authors believe are mobilizable before M + 120. Most are motorized rifle units; probably fewer than ten are armored divisions. Category III formations muster an M-day personnel strength of only 25 percent and have but one-half of their required equipment, virtually all of which is in storage. With respect to tanks, artillery, and armored personnel carriers, the other 50 percent is obtainable only from current production or, as is more likely, from stockpiles of older and less battle-worthy equipment. As for additional "soft" (unarmored) vehicles, they would be drawn primarily from civilian resources. Thus even a fully mobilized Category III division would be seri-

---

rity and to keep an eye on the loyalty of the Czechoslovak armed forces and police, whose reliability and morale leave much to be desired from the Soviet point of view." Malcolm Mackintosh, *The Evolution of the Warsaw Pact,* Adelphi Papers, 58 (London: International Institute for Strategic Studies, June 1969), p. 16.

18. It is probably because of this, as well as because of a desire to retain a military "window" on a post-Tito Yugoslavia, that the USSR has been so reluctant to permit its forces in Hungary to be the subject of MBFR negotiations.

19. For an informative sketch of the readiness of Soviet reserves, see Irving Heymont and Melvin H. Rosen, "Five Foreign Army Reserve Systems," *Military Review,* Vol. 53 (March 1973).

ously deficient in both high quality combat equipment and durable logistics support vehicles.

In sum, the unreadiness of many Soviet formations, the demonstrated weaknesses of the Red Army's logistics infrastructure, and the burden of maintaining two separate and mutually nonsupporting fronts (Central Europe and the Far East)—all serve to constrain the amount of military power the USSR could quickly bring to bear opposite NATO Center. Two other aspects of the Soviet military threat that also merit attention are the generally recognized qualitative inferiority of some major Soviet weapons systems compared to those of NATO and the need for Soviet forces to muster a large numerical advantage over NATO if they were to undertake a major offensive.

The USSR's quantitative superiority in tanks, for example, is offset at least partially not only by NATO's formidable anti-tank defenses but also by the greater durability, long-range gun accuracy, and armor protection of NATO tanks. Moreover, as is shown in Table 2-3, the T-62, which currently forms the backbone of Soviet armor, lacks the weight (protection) of most NATO tanks. Also, most Soviet tactical aircraft are markedly inferior in quality to those of NATO.

The size of Soviet forces must, in addition, be viewed within the context in which they are likely to be used. Offensive operations generally require forces greater than those of the defending enemy; indeed, conventional military wisdom has long held that attainment of at least a three-to-one theater-level numerical advantage over a determined defender is necessary before an attacker can count on reasonably quick success. Recently some analysts have suggested that NATO's relatively thin defensive screen along the Central Front and the danger for both

Table 2-3. Comparison of First-Line Soviet and NATO Medium Tanks, by Weight, Horsepower, Speed, and Armament

Characteristic	*T-62*	*Chieftain*	*AMX-30*	*Leopard*	*M-60A1*	*M-60A2*[a]
Country of manufacture	USSR	U.K.	France	West Germany	U.S.	U.S.
Combat weight (tons)	40	62	40	44	53	57
Power plant (horsepower)	580	720	710	830	750	750
Maximum speed (miles per hour)	30	30	40	41	30	30
Primary armament (guntube millimeter)	115	120	105	105	105	152
Secondary armament (number of machine guns)	2	3	2	2	2	2
Year introduced	1965	1966	1967	1965	1962	1973

Sources: "Comparative Characteristics of Main Battle Tanks" (U.S. Army Armor School, Fort Knox, Kentucky, June 1973; processed), p. 18-1; and International Institute for Strategic Studies, *The Military Balance 1972–1973*, p. 74.

a. The M-60A2 is armed with the Shillelagh, a 152 mm tube capable of firing either conventional high explosive rounds or a Shillelagh anti-tank missile. Current plans call for the procurement of about five hundred units to supplement U.S. main battle tanks.

sides of concentrating ground forces in a potentially nuclear environment might permit the Red Army to overrun NATO Center with only a two-to-one superiority. Yet, as is indicated later in this study, the Soviet Union and its allies are unlikely at any stage of mobilization to generate *in the Central Region as a whole* more than a two-to-one advantage over NATO in combat aircraft, combat troops, and total deployed military manpower. What is ominous for NATO is that in key sectors along the Central Front the Pact has an advantage over NATO of three to one or better, based on current and projected dispositions. (See Appendix D.)

Tactical Air Forces

The USSR has the largest number of tactical combat aircraft of any country in the world—some 9,200 planes divided between the Soviet Tactical Air Force and the Air Defense Command.[20] This impressive number, however, is offset somewhat by the generally higher quality of aircraft at NATO's disposal.

On balance, Western aircraft, and particularly U.S.-made aircraft, such as the F-4 Phantom, have greater durability, range, and payload and more advanced fire control systems than do modern Soviet planes, such as the MIG-21 and MIG-23 interceptors and the SU-7 and SU-11 fighter bombers. Also American and Western European pilots are distinctly better trained, and many have had considerable combat experience.[21]

20. Data on Soviet aircraft in this section are from T. N. Dupuy and Wendell Blanchard, *The Almanac of World Military Power* (R. R. Bowker Company, 1972), pp. 150, 152.

21. Historically the combat performance of both Soviet pilots and Soviet tactical aircraft has been markedly inferior to that of Russia's enemies. In the Second World War, Soviet aircraft losses during the first six days of the German invasion of the USSR (June 21–26, 1941) totaled some 3,800 planes, 1,000 of which were destroyed in the air. Luftwaffe losses during the same period were 121 aircraft. In the Korean War, Soviet-built aircraft (mostly MIG-15s and later some MIG-17s), many of them flown by Russian pilots drawn from elite Soviet Air Force units, were downed in aerial combat at the lopsided rate of almost 14 planes for every aircraft lost by the United States. In air combat over the Suez Canal from July 1967 to October 1973 and over North Vietnam from 1965 through 1972, Soviet aircraft again suffered comparatively greater losses although in Indochina the kill ratio vis-à-vis the United States was only 2.5 to 1. It should be noted, however, that past performance, Soviet air doctrine, and the size of Russia's tactical air forces clearly suggest that the USSR not only is prepared to sustain disproportionate losses in the air but also is capable of replacing them.

The Soviets' extraordinary emphasis on strategic air defense, which serves to constrain the number of aircraft that might be available for combat in the Central Region, is as important to NATO as Russia's qualitative inferiority. About 4,000 Soviet tactical aircraft are interceptor/fighters, oriented primarily toward the defense of Russia itself. In the event of war a portion of these aircraft, most of which (about 3,200) are part of the Air Defense Command, would probably be assigned to combat missions against NATO; the bulk, however, would in all likelihood be retained in the Soviet Union as a hedge against a strategic strike on Russia by the United States. Thus perhaps 6,000 to 7,000 aircraft, including a large number of obsolescent MIG-17, MIG-19, and Il-28 planes, constitute the potential Soviet tactical air threat confronting NATO.

Yet even if all Soviet "air defense" interceptors were withheld from combat, the USSR alone could still field about as many tactical aircraft in the Central Region as could NATO. (See Table 4-1 in Chapter 4 below.) Moreover, although few Soviet aircraft are designed exclusively for close support of troops engaged on thc ground, most are capable of performing this role with varying degrees of effectiveness. Indeed, most Soviet tactical aircraft not allocated to air defense are oriented toward the achievement of local air superiority *over the battlefield,* a mission clearly supportive of the short-war doctrine of the Soviet Union. In sharp contrast is the tactical air posture of the United States, which relies on fewer but much more expensive multipurpose aircraft geared to the time-consuming attainment of theater-level air superiority as a prerequisite to a deep interdiction campaign, which presupposes a more protracted conflict.

Moreover, while the number of airfields on the continent that are suitable for use by most NATO aircraft is less than 100, East Germany, Czechoslovakia, and Poland alone provide the Pact with 220 airfields that are capable of handling high-performance aircraft, plus another 140 runways suitable for less sophisticated planes.[22] The impressive number of Pact airfields and their pervasive dispersal throughout Eastern Europe and Western Russia constitute a formidable obstacle to any attempt on the part of NATO to achieve the kind of air supremacy present Western tactical air doctrine so strongly emphasizes.

22. Neville Brown, *European Security 1972–1980* (London: Royal United Services Institute for Defense Studies, 1972), p. 124.

Table 2-4. Eastern European Ground Forces, by Number and Type

	Type of division			
Country	*Motorized rifle*[a]	*Tank*[a]	*Other*	*Total*
East Germany	4	2	...	6
Poland	8 (3)	5 (2)	2	15
Czechoslovakia	5 (1)	5	$\frac{1}{3}$[b]	$10\frac{1}{3}$
Hungary	4 (1)	2 (1)	$\frac{1}{6}$[b]	$6\frac{1}{6}$
Rumania	7	2	$1\frac{1}{2}$[b]	$10\frac{1}{2}$
Bulgaria	8 (3)	$1\frac{2}{3}$[b]	$\frac{1}{6}$[b]	$9\frac{5}{6}$
Total	36	$17\frac{2}{3}$	$4\frac{1}{6}$	$57\frac{5}{6}$

Sources: International Institute for Strategic Studies, *The Military Balance 1972–1973*, pp. 10–13; and Dupuy and Blanchard, *The Almanac of World Military Power*, pp. 131–45.

a. Numbers in parentheses refer to skeletal divisions or division equivalents, included in total.

b. Represents division equivalents and includes airborne, amphibious assault, artillery, and mountain formations.

Eastern European Military Capabilities

European allies of the Soviet Union ostensibly account for about one-third of the Warsaw Pact's total military power. Their contribution to the Pact's war-fighting potential, however, is marginal. Low levels of readiness and inferior arms characterize most Eastern European armies. More important, it is highly doubtful that certain Pact members would participate in any combat operations other than local ones in defense of their respective homelands.

On paper, the combined forces of East Germany, Poland, Czechoslovakia, Hungary, Rumania, and Bulgaria are impressive. (See Table 2-4.) Together, these countries muster about fifty-eight divisions and almost 2,500 combat aircraft. Yet armored divisions number less than eighteen, of which at least three are believed to be skeletal formations; the bulk of the remaining forty divisions are of the motorized-rifle type, and many, if not most, are substantially under strength. Thus perhaps no more than thirty-five Eastern European divisions may be considered combat ready.

Aging and in many cases antiquated equipment further reduces the potential effectiveness of Eastern European armed forces. For example, although increasing numbers of Soviet T-62 main battle tanks are being delivered to the USSR's continental allies, the mainstay of non-Soviet Pact armor is still the T-55, supplemented by sizable inventories of the

Table 2-5. Eastern European Tactical Combat Aircraft, First-Line and Obsolescent

Country	*First-line*	*Obsolescent*[a]	*Total*
East Germany	390	40	430
Poland	220	525	745
Czechoslovakia	400	220	620
Hungary	140	40	180
Rumania	100	150	250
Bulgaria	84	180	264
Total	1,334	1,155	2,489

Source: Dupuy and Blanchard, *The Almanac of World Military Power*, pp. 131–45.
a. Includes all Ilyushin-28 tactical light bombers and MIG-15 and MIG-17 fighters, first introduced into service in 1949–50, 1948, and 1953, respectively.

even older T-54s.[23] The ancient T-34/85, first introduced into service on the Russian Front in 1943, is still widely used for training purposes.

Eastern European air forces are similarly plagued by dependence on obsolescent equipment. As is shown in Table 2-5, about one-half of non-Soviet Pact tactical combat aircraft (no Eastern European country has strategic aircraft) are Il-28s, MIG-15s, or MIG-17s—all of which represent designs that are two decades old or more. The contribution of these subsonic machines to the Pact's overall tactical air capabilities is certainly less than that provided by the more modern MIG-19, MIG-21, and SU-7 aircraft, which constitute the core of Eastern European combat air power. It is significant that, as far as is known, no continental ally of the USSR has yet acquired the formidable single-seat tactical fighter SU-11 or the two latest models in the MIG series—the MIG-23 and the MIG-25.

The relative military weakness of non-Soviet Pact armed forces is compounded by the doubtful availability of some contingents for offensive operations across the Central Front. In truth, it is the dubious *political* reliability and not the questionable combat effectiveness of Eastern European armies that raises the most doubts as to their value to the USSR.

It is highly unlikely that Soviet forces invading NATO Center would be accompanied by more than token formations from most of the Eastern European countries. Only the armies of Poland and Stalinist East Germany are likely to appear in force—the East German because of the DDR's unregenerate loyalty to Moscow and its obvious stake in the outcome of hostilities in West Germany, and the Polish because its location astride major Soviet lines of communication and supply would make

23. The T-55 was first introduced into service in 1962; the T-54 in 1954.

it difficult for Poland to avoid participation. The Polish Army, the largest and best-equipped in Eastern Europe, fields sizable amphibious assault and airborne formations, whose very existence implies that they were designed to supplement the Soviet Union's offensive potential.

There are a number of reasons for the Soviet Union to expect little help from the rest of its allies.

1. Nowhere in the Warsaw Treaty is there an obligation to participate in combat operations outside the Treaty area, nor are there indications that any Eastern European country so construes the Treaty.

2. A desire to preclude, or at least to limit, NATO retaliation against the Pact countries would probably deter some of the latter from anything more than pro forma support of a Soviet offensive. That desire is reinforced by a very real fear that NATO, in trying to limit the scope of hostilities (as prescribed by the doctrine of flexible response), might forgo retaliation against the Soviet Union in exchange for disproportionately heavy strikes against Eastern European countries participating in the attack, as well as against Soviet forces within those countries.

3. Antagonisms between the USSR and Eastern European countries, and among these countries, virtually rule out certain member states as partners in a Soviet-sponsored war against NATO. It would be a mistake to assume that the ostensible commonality of interests underlying Eastern Europe's peacetime obedience to the Pact's Soviet-controlled Joint High Command would survive a severe crisis or the outbreak of hostilities.

It is unlikely that Rumania, for example, which fields some 10 percent of the combat aircraft and more than 20 percent of the combat-ready Eastern European divisions theoretically available to the Pact, would even consider participating in an invasion of the Central Front. Indeed, Rumanian President Nicolae Ceausescu not only has publicly denounced the Warsaw Pact as an "anachronism" in an era of "*détente,* cooperation and peace,"[24] but also has prohibited Soviet forces from conducting military exercises on Rumanian territory.[25] As for Bulgaria, its small and poorly equipped forces are distant from the Central Front and remain oriented exclusively toward the Bosporus area.

The reliability of Czech and Hungarian forces is equally dubious; resurgent nationalism in both countries and the demonstrated sympathy

24. Interview with Strobe Talbott in *Time* (April 2, 1973), p. 32.

25. In 1972, however, Soviet forces were permitted to cross Rumanian territory in order to take part in an exercise in Bulgaria.

of their armies toward past anti-Soviet regimes would make them at least unwilling candidates for an attack on Western Europe. Nonetheless, since the 200-mile West German-Czech border constitutes the southern half of the Central Front and thus would in all probability be the locus of heavy combat, it is prudent to assume that most Czech forces would be engaged, if only in economy-of-force operations.

In sum, a politically realistic assessment of the prospects for participation by Eastern European countries in an invasion of NATO Center strongly suggests that Hungarian, Rumanian, and Bulgarian forces may be excluded entirely and that the most the Soviet Union could count on would be the East German, Czech, and Polish armies and their tactical air forces.

CHAPTER THREE

NATO AND THE U.S. CONTRIBUTION TO THE CENTRAL REGION'S DEFENSE

U.S. forces are but one of many allied military contingents assigned to the defense of NATO's Central Region. Any discussion of U.S. forces would thus be incomplete without an assessment of the broader alliance of which they are a part.

NATO's Central Region: Command Structure and Geography

The Central Region of NATO is within the purview of the European Command, which in turn is under the direction of the Supreme Allied Commander, Europe (SACEUR). The Center is one of three regions for which SACEUR has military responsibility in wartime. The other two are the Northern Region (embracing Norway, Denmark, and Schleswig-Holstein, the northernmost state of the Federal Republic of Germany [FRG]), and the Southern Region, encompassing Italy, Greece, Turkey, and the Mediterranean. The Central Region is officially designated AFCENT (Allied Forces Central Europe) and embraces the Netherlands, Belgium, Luxembourg, and the FRG (excluding Schleswig-Holstein). France, though not formally contributing forces to NATO, is geographically inseparable from AFCENT. Noncontinental members of the alliance contributing forces to AFCENT are Canada, the United Kingdom, and the United States. The primary wartime mission of AFCENT forces is to conduct a successful forward defense of the Central Region.

In pursuit of that mission, AFCENT ground forces are organized into two army groups: the Northern Army Group (NORTHAG) and the Central Army Group (CENTAG). NORTHAG has four corps containing in all eleven divisions, which occupy a front along the border between the Elbe River in the north and Göttingen-Cologne in the south. CENTAG fields four corps containing thirteen and two-thirds divisions, disposed from a contiguous boundary with NORTHAG in the north to the Austrian and Swiss borders in the south. (See Figure 3-1.)

NORTHAG's four corps are Dutch, West German, British, and Belgian, and they are disposed (in that order, north to south) along a front of about 400 kilometers (250 miles) measured at the border. Of CENTAG's four corps, two are U.S. and two West German. The West German corps are positioned on each flank of CENTAG and are contiguous with the Belgian corps in the north and along the southern border of West Germany. The two U.S. corps are located primarily in the center of CENTAG, astride the major approaches to Frankfurt and Nuremberg. The length of CENTAG's frontage at the border is about 600 kilometers (375 miles). The thirteen and two-thirds divisions in CENTAG include the two French divisions in West Germany and the equivalent of one-third of a Canadian division. Neither the Canadians nor the French occupy forward positions, and the latter of course are not formally at the disposal of the Commanding General, CENTAG. The eleven divisions in NORTHAG include all Dutch, West German, British, and Belgian forces earmarked for that command, although some are not currently on line at the border.

The terrain and demography of NATO Center vary considerably. From the Elbe River in the north to the Harz Mountains near the NORTHAG-CENTAG boundary, the land is generally flat or gently rolling and is crisscrossed by numerous small water obstacles. The north-south road network in this area is excellent, although from east to west it is less extensive. About sixty miles west of the border, the land is very flat and low, with many canals and rivers. As one approaches the Rhine River, small communities and farmlands give way to large cities and major industrial concentrations in the Ruhr River basin and along the North Sea coast. This northern portion of the Central Region is known as the North German Plain and is considered the most favorable route for a Warsaw Pact attack, because of its flat and open terrain, excellent network of roads, and proximity to the coast and to major communications centers along the Rhine. (See Figure 3-2.) From the Harz Mountains southward (the CENTAG area), the initial line of contact would be along a mountainous and wooded border with only two narrow potential corridors of invasion: the Fulda Gap, aimed at the Frankfurt area, and the broader, more open approach from the Thuringer Mountain-Hof area to Wurzburg and Nuremberg. Along the border areas in this region, the terrain is rough, heavily wooded, and crisscrossed by streams and small rivers. The east-west road network is generally good, but distances to the Rhine from this sector are considerably greater than from the sector to the north. Most roads are sandwiched in between the surrounding hills and mountains. The CENTAG area is therefore more favorable to the defense than NORTHAG.

NATO's Central Region: Allied Capabilities

Allied ground and tactical air forces represent the principal elements of NATO's capacity to defend Western Europe in its Central Region.

Ground Forces

The collective order of battle for all non-U.S. NATO ground forces committed to the defense of the Central Region is detailed in Table 3-1. Together with U.S. forces, they form the conventional shield against which Warsaw Pact forces would be directed in the event of hostilities. European capabilities are impressive; with the addition of U.S. forces they are formidable. The combined strength of the armies of the six non-U.S. participants in the Central Region's defense is about 1 million men. This figure is only slightly less than the 1.1 million effectives the authors believe would be available to the Warsaw Pact for combat in the Central Region by M + 30. (See Chapter 4, Table 4-1.) It is not at all certain, however, that the organization, structure, and disposition of European and particularly U.S. forces are optimally geared to meet the requirements of a short, intense war.

America's NATO allies have provided the equivalent of about twenty and one-third divisions for immediate commitment to the Central Region. Eleven are positioned in NORTHAG and about nine and one-third in CENTAG (the remaining four and one-third in CENTAG are U.S. divisions). Many are substantially understrength and would need fillers from reserve organizations or from other regular units within the first few days of mobilization. Western European divisions earmarked for the Center are mostly mechanized and contain substantial numbers of tanks although NATO's marked numerical inferiority in tanks is an acknowledged weakness. NATO has attempted to redress the imbalance

Figure 3-1. NATO Center

Figure 3-2. Most Likely and Least Likely Routes for Invasion of NATO Center

Table 3-1. Current Ground Force Order of Battle for European and Canadian NATO Members Contributing to the Defense of the Central Region[a]

Belgium

Active army strength: 71,500
Committed to NATO Center:[b] 1 corps consisting of 1 armored brigade, 3 motorized infantry brigades, 2 reconnaissance battalions, 1 paracommando regiment
Other active formations:[c] 6 infantry battalions for territorial defense
Army reserves: 120,000 ready reservists to form 1 mechanized brigade, various logistics support and independent territorial defense units, plus 500,000 trained reservists as replacements

Canada

Active army strength: 33,000
Committed to NATO Center:[b] 1 mechanized combat group consisting of 3 infantry battalions, 1 reconnaissance regiment, 1 light artillery battalion
Other active formations:[c] 2 mechanized combat groups, 1 airborne regiment, 1 air-mobile combat group[d]
Army reserves: 19,000 organized for mobilization on short notice

France[e]

Active army strength: 328,000
Committed to NATO Center:[b] 1 corps of the First Army consisting of 2 mechanized divisions (in Federal Republic of Germany)
Other active formations:[c] remainder of First Army, consisting of 3 mechanized divisions (in France); Strategic Reserve, consisting of 2 airborne brigades, 1 motorized brigade (air transportable); and Territorial Defense Force, consisting of 2 alpine brigades, 2 motorized infantry regiments, 4 armored car regiments, 1 parachute battalion, 25 infantry battalions
Army reserves: 450,000 trained reservists; part of these make up 80 infantry battalions and 5 armored car regiments

Federal Republic of Germany[f]

Active army strength: 327,000
Committed to NATO Center:[b] 3 corps consisting of 11 divisions (12th division with northern flank units)
Other active formations:[c] Territorial Army consisting of 6 home defense groups, 300 motorized security companies, various combat support and service units
Army reserves: 1.8 million reservists; 540,000 available for immediate mobilization

The Netherlands

Active army strength: 76,000
Committed to NATO Center:[b] 1 corps consisting of 2 armored brigades, 4 mechanized brigades
Other active formations:[c] small number of regular army units for territorial defense
Army reserves: 350,000 trained reservists; 40,000 available for immediate mobilization to form 1 infantry division plus corps support troops

United Kingdom

Active army strength: 176,500

Committed to NATO Center:[b] British Army of the Rhine, consisting of 1 corps of 3 divisions

Other active formations:[c] U.K. land forces made up of Strategic Reserve, consisting of 1 division and 1 commando regiment, and the U.K. Command, consisting of 18 infantry battalions

Army reserves: 120,000 Regular Army Reserves with specific mobilization assignments; 177,000 Army General Reserves used as general replacements; and 56,400 Territorial and Army Volunteer Reserves formed into combat and support units for home defense or for the British Army of the Rhine

Sources: Authors' estimates based on material appearing in T. N. Dupuy and Wendell Blanchard, *The Almanac of World Military Power*, 2d ed. (T. N. Dupuy Associates, 1972); International Institute for Strategic Studies, *The Military Balance 1972–1973* (London: IISS, 1972); *White Paper 1971/1972: The Security of the Federal Republic of Germany and the Development of the Federal Armed Forces*, published in Bonn by the Federal Minister of Defense on behalf of the German Federal Government (1971); *French White Paper on National Defense*, Vol. 1 (New York: Ambassade de France, Service de Presse et d'Information, 1972); Donald S. MacDonald, Minister of National Defence, *Defence in the 70's: White Paper on Defence* (Ottawa: Information Canada, 1971); "For the First Time—A Distinctly Canadian Approach," and "Canadian Forces Combat Strength," *Armed Forces Journal International*, Vol. 110 (April 1973); "The Royal Air Force," and "The British Army," *Armed Forces Journal International*, Vol. 110 (May 1973); *The Force Structure in the Federal Republic of Germany: Analysis and Options: Summary* (Report of the Force Structure Commission to the Government of the Federal Republic of Germany, 1972).

a. For details on each country see Appendix A.

b. Includes the major ground force units earmarked for NATO in the Central Region (AFCENT) in the event of hostilities. All are on the continent with the exception of several U.K. units from the British Army of the Rhine currently on duty in Northern Ireland. Each corps (except the French) is on line at the West German border; however, some units (for example, Belgian brigades) are not in position.

c. These are major allied ground force units not at present committed to NATO Center. They remain under national command and could be committed to the Central Region, depending on the situation. (See Appendix A.)

d. Designated for use on the northern flank.

e. France, although not a formal contributor to NATO, is included because the authors believe France would fight on the side of its allies in NATO in the event of an attack on NATO Center. (See the discussion on page 34.)

f. The FRG structure is based on the recommendations of the Force Structure Commission. (See Sources above.)

by procuring larger quantities of sophisticated anti-tank weapons and by qualitative improvements of its own tanks over those of the Pact. Since anti-tank systems are distinctly more advantageous in a defensive than in an offensive role, their proliferation and use suit NATO deployments and serve to free its smaller tank forces for optimum use in the counterattack role at decisive points.

Table 3-1 shows that sizable regular ground forces remain under national command; they would probably be available to NATO in the event of a Pact invasion. The same is true of Army reserves. There are approximately 3.5 million trained Army reservists among the six allied nations participating in the defense of the Central Region. Of these, some 35 to 40 percent (1.2 million to 1.4 million men) are immediately available to form new units or act as fillers for cadre-strength regular formations. A conservative estimate, discussed in Appendix A, is that if national command forces and readily available Army reserves were utilized, at least fifteen and two-thirds additional divisions could be committed to NATO Center by U.S. allies within sixty days of mobilization.

France has been included as a NATO partner in all force calculations. France remains a member of the Atlantic Alliance and continues to station two mechanized divisions in West Germany while maintaining close liaison with NATO headquarters.[1] Certainly no prudent Warsaw Pact military planner could ignore the strong probability that France would participate in a conflict in the Central Region. There is ample evidence to support the presumption of French involvement. President de Gaulle, in a letter to President Johnson on March 7, 1966, following the former's announcement of France's intention to end its participation in certain NATO activities, said that France remained "determined to fight beside her allies if one of them should suffer unprovoked aggression." A French diplomatic note to the United States two weeks later indicated that France would participate if Article 5 of the Treaty of Washington were invoked. However, France reserved the right to decide, at the time of aggression, whether in light of its own interests involvement was justified—an option which, of course, is open to all members of the alliance under Article 5. Indeed, no less an unreconstructed Gaullist than former French Defense Minister Michel Debré, in a major statement of French defense policy in October 1971, concluded that France

> must take part in the balance and the peace in Europe and around Europe. In other words, national defense does not simply mean defense of the land. France is part of a whole, and the status of this whole is of major importance for her destiny. . . . One can hardly imagine deterrence in reference to our territory being credible, were we to remain passive in the face of threats which, though hanging over countries or peoples beyond our own frontier, would however affect us directly. It is here that one can see clearly that a nation such as France is not neutral and cannot be neutral.[2]

Tactical Air Forces

The tactical air forces of U.S. allies contributing to the defense of the Central Region total some 2,100 fighter-attack aircraft, most of which

1. France's so-called withdrawal from NATO in 1966 consisted of (1) withdrawal of French personnel from NATO's integrated Military Headquarters, (2) termination of the assignment of French forces to the international commands, and (3) removal from French territory of the International Headquarters and other facilities not under French control.

2. Michel Debré, in an address delivered at the Institut des Hautes Etudes de Défense Nationale, October 19, 1971.

are employable either in the air superiority role or, to a lesser degree, in close support of ground forces. Approximately 20 to 25 percent of the total inventory is obsolescent, comparable to such Warsaw Pact aircraft as the MIG-15 and the MIG-17.

The largest number of these fighter aircraft are American-designed F-104s. Capable of Mach 2.2 speed at high altitudes, the G model was assembled in Europe under an intra-European production program involving West Germany, Italy, Belgium, and the Netherlands. The F-104, although officially characterized as a multimission aircraft, is decidedly deficient in the close support role since it was designed as an interceptor with optimum performance at high altitudes. Equipped with air-to-air missiles, the F-104 is a match in air-to-air combat for all but the most advanced fighters. About one-half of the Belgian and approximately 80 percent of the Dutch fighter fleets consist of F-104s. The three Canadian fighter-attack squadrons in Europe are composed of F-104s, as are over one-half of West German fighter squadrons.

French squadrons are equipped primarily with the Mirage III, an all-weather aircraft similar in performance to the F-104, and the Mystère IVA, a near-supersonic aircraft considered to be obsolescent against any first-line Pact fighter. In the hands of Israeli pilots, however, the Mystère did perform very well against the MIG-15 and MIG-17 during the Arab-Israeli War of 1967. The Mirage is reputed to be capable of operating from short, unprepared airstrips, whereas the other first-line fighters are not. Belgium is the only other Western European country with Mirages in its operational squadrons. The United Kingdom uses a large number of American-built F-4 Phantoms, the late models of which are probably the most versatile performers of any fighters in the world. Other first-line British aircraft include the heavily armed, supersonic Lightning fighter and the subsonic Buccaneer and Harrier, which are suited for ground attack roles. The Harrier has both a vertical takeoff and landing (VTOL) and a short strip (STOL) capability, although in the former mode it is less well armed and has a shorter operating range. The Federal Republic of Germany, in a recent effort to modernize its fighter fleet, has initiated a program to procure late models of the F-4 Phantom.

Thus, although the number of aircraft in allied air fleets is less than that in the fleets of Warsaw Pact countries, this numerical inferiority is substantially offset by the generally greater versatility, combat radius, and payload of NATO aircraft. Moreover, the obsolescent portion of NATO's tactical air forces is much smaller than that of the Pact.

The principal weakness of NATO's tactical air forces is their limited ability to provide close support for ground forces, a critical need in the early stages of hostilities, when NATO's combat formations would be outnumbered and outgunned on the ground. Less than 20 percent of allied aircraft are designed primarily for attacking ground targets, the remainder being multimission aircraft designed mainly for the air superiority mission.

The U.S. Contribution to the Defense of the Central Region

In accordance with U.S. strategic guidance, which assigns top priority to a forward conventional defense of Europe in conjunction with allied forces on the continent, America's general purpose forces are structured and equipped primarily for European contingencies. Table 3-2 lists U.S. land and air general purpose forces by type, size, and location.

Ground Forces

Of the Army's thirteen active divisions, four and one-third are forward-deployed in the Central Region (West Germany), and another three and two-thirds are stationed in the United States and earmarked for Europe. Two and two-thirds of these earmarked divisions are designed for rapid deployment to Europe. They are "dual based"; that is, additional sets of equipment are prepositioned in Europe for these divisions. Other equipment and facilities for their initial support in combat have also been set aside in Europe to augment the line of communications there. Thus the active Army commitment, which constitutes the core of the U.S. contribution to the defense of NATO Center, consists of eight divisions (four armored and four mechanized), together with their supporting forces. The Army's remaining five active divisions are located in the United States and in Asia. Three are stationed in the continental United States as a strategic reserve for Asian and other contingencies, and two are forward-deployed in the Pacific—one in the Republic of Korea, and the other in Hawaii. All five are infantry-heavy divisions but could be deployed to Europe during the later stages of mobilization.

Major reserve component units of the Army include eight divisions and twenty-one separate brigades. Of the divisions, three (two armored and one mechanized) are structurally better suited for European con-

Table 3-2. Current U.S. Defense Posture, Ground and Tactical Air Forces, Fiscal Year 1974[a]

Ground forces

Active Army (785,000)

Deployed in Europe

2	armored divisions
2⅓	mechanized divisions

Oriented to Europe, based in continental U.S.

2	armored divisions
1⅔	mechanized divisions

Deployed in Asia (Korea)

1	infantry division

Oriented to Asia, based in continental U.S. and Hawaii

2	infantry divisions

Strategic Reserve, based in continental U.S.

1	airborne division
1	airmobile division

Army Reserve (714,000)

1	mechanized division
2	armored divisions
5	infantry divisions
4	mechanized brigades
1	armored brigade
18	infantry brigades
1	airborne brigade
155	battalions

Active Marine Corps (197,000)

1	division, based on U.S. East Coast
1	division, based on U.S. West Coast
1	division, deployed in Pacific area

Marine Corps Reserve (46,000)

1	division

Tactical air forces[b]

Active (692,000)

Deployed in Europe

8	fighter wings
1	fighter squadron
2	reconnaissance wings
2	airlift wings

These 13 units include approximately 500 fighter/attack, 100 reconnaissance, and 90 airlift aircraft

Tactical Air Command, based in continental U.S. (Ninth and Twelfth Air Forces)

11	fighter wings
1	fighter squadron[c]
2	reconnaissance wings
5	airlift wings[c]

These 19 units include approximately 700 fighter/attack, 100 reconnaissance, and 240 airlift aircraft

1	special operations wing

Table 3-2 *(continued)*

Deployed in Asia/Pacific
- 7 fighter wings[d]
- 1 reconnaissance wing
- 1 airlift wing

These 9 units include approximately 350 fighter/attack, 50 reconnaissance, and 50 airlift aircraft

- 1 special operations wing

Reserve (346,000)[e]
- 30 fighter groups (squadrons)
- 7 reconnaissance groups (squadrons)
- 37 airlift groups (squadrons)
- 1 bomber group

These 75 units include approximately 750 fighter/attack, 950 other tactical, and 600 other aircraft

Sources: International Institute for Strategic Studies, *The Military Balance 1972–1973;* "Military Manpower Requirements Report for FY 1974" (U.S. Department of Defense, February 1973; processed); "U.S. Air Force Almanac," "Pacific Air Forces," "United States Air Forces in Europe," "Tactical Air Command," "Air Force Reserve," and "Air National Guard," in *Air Force Magazine*, Vol. 56 (May 1973); and authors' estimates based on unclassified material from the U.S. Department of Defense.

a. The table includes only major combat and direct support forces. Worldwide dispositions are shown. Some units not deployed or oriented to NATO could be used there as required. For example, the mobility of tactical air forces permits rapid deployment to Europe of units not formally allocated for European tactical air contingencies.

b. Includes only major combat and support units. Major headquarters units, airbase wings, and some special units (for example, electronic warfare, air rescue and air refueling units, and training wings) are not included. Some wing headquarters do not have a full complement of aircraft.

c. The tactical fighter squadron and one tactical airlift wing under operational control of the Strategic Air Command.

d. Two wings deployed temporarily from Tactical Air Command under Pacific Air Force operational control.

e. Air Reserve and Air National Guard groups reflect headquarters designations. The number of aircraft in a group is similar to that in a squadron.

tingencies than for combat elsewhere. The remaining reserve divisions, all of them infantry, and the separate brigades, most of which are infantry, provide a flexible strategic reserve, a portion of which could be sent to Europe if needed. A long time is required at present to mobilize reserve formations and bring them up to sufficient combat readiness for European deployment. Even if mobilization were to precede a conflict by several weeks, the present unreadiness of most reserve units is so pronounced that it is highly unlikely they could be mobilized and deployed in time to affect significantly the outcome of a short war in Europe.

The Marine Corps' three active and one reserve divisions are additional U.S. ground forces that are potentially available to NATO. Each division has its own air wing. Of the three active divisions, one is located on the East Coast of the United States and contains two battalion landing teams afloat with naval forces operating in the Mediterranean and the Caribbean. Although the division is explicitly oriented toward the littorals of either NATO flank, in an emergency it could be released to

SACEUR for deployment with the Allied Command Europe Mobile Force. The other two active Marine divisions and air wings are oriented toward the Pacific (one on the U.S. West Coast and one forward-deployed in Japan, Okinawa, and Hawaii) and structured for Asian contingencies, although the division on the West Coast could, if necessary, be deployed to Europe. The Marine Reserve division and air wing are mobilizable in a much shorter time than are Army reserve component divisions, primarily because in the Marines active and reserve components are integrated at low levels of command. When mobilized, the Marine Reserve division could be committed to Europe or be added to the strategic reserve as a hedge against minor contingencies that might arise elewhere at the same time.

U.S. ground forces currently deployed in the Central Region consist of two armored divisions and two and one-third mechanized divisions of the U.S. Seventh Army plus their associated combat support forces and logistics bases. All combat forces are organized into two U.S. Army Corps (V and VII Corps) located in CENTAG astride major avenues of approach running from the border toward the Frankfurt-Darmstadt area and through Nuremberg toward the Stuttgart-Heidelberg area. It is important to recognize that the location of U.S. forces in southern Germany instead of the more crucial North German Plain is less a function of contemporary military realities than a legacy of post–World War II occupation agreements between the United States, Great Britain, France, and the Soviet Union.

The major peacetime line of communication (LOC) supporting U.S. forces originates at the West German port city of Bremerhaven and moves southward along the major highway and rail networks to the northern boundary of U.S. dispositions, thence to installations and depots throughout the two corps areas of the Seventh Army. (See Figure 3-1.) This Bremerhaven LOC is more than 250 highway miles long and at some points closely skirts the East German border.

Most prepositioned equipment (a total of about two and two-thirds division sets) located in the NATO Central Region for rapid deployment of Army reinforcements from the United States is in three major depots. One of these is supposed to contain 50 percent or more of the designated stocks. Another serious problem is the concentration of a single class of supply or unique items in one or two depots. For tactical and administrative reasons, the depots are very near or west of the Rhine River. Access to some of the depots is restricted to one major route, so that it would be difficult to rapidly forward-deploy forces that had collected their equipment at the site. Moreover, troop columns assembled at the site and on the constricted, lengthy road net toward forward areas would be extremely vulnerable to air attack. Most of the equipment at the depots is unprotected and is arranged in concentrated patterns spread over extended areas.

The medium tank strength of the four and one-third U.S. divisions deployed in Europe, together with those considered immediately available to allied forces, numbers about 6,700. This figure falls far short of the approximately 11,800 tanks that are immediately available to Warsaw Pact divisions.[3] The Pact's advantage would increase as mobilization proceeded, reaching a superiority of almost three to one by M + 60. (See Chapter 4, Table 4-1.) The relative inferiority of NATO tank strength is partially offset, however, by the alliance's formidable anti-tank defenses. As was noted earlier, anti-tank weapons in defensive operations can be used to wear down attacking tank forces and to permit the defender to pool his own tanks for counterattacks. Moreover, new developments in anti-tank technology,[4] as was shown in the Mideast war of 1973, offer "the possibility not only of inflicting severe losses on the enemy armored forces but also of imposing considerable delays on their advance and so providing more time for redeployment and reinforcement moves."[5] U.S. forces structured for European contingencies are amply equipped with anti-tank weapons. For example, each mechanized battalion has twenty-seven DRAGON and eighteen TOW anti-tank missile launchers. These and other systems are highly accurate at distances extending from near point-blank range to more than 2,500 meters.

The issue of the ratio of combat to support manpower in U.S. forces deployed in and oriented to European contingencies continues to be a major concern of critics who see excessive manpower resources used to support the combat soldier and who seek to reduce as much support

3. Sources of immediately available tanks are: for NATO, tanks of the Belgian, Dutch, and West German armies, tanks of British, French, and Canadian contingents in West Germany, and tanks in the two U.S. armored and two and one-third mechanized divisions in West Germany; for the Warsaw Pact, the tanks of twenty-seven Soviet divisions in Poland, Czechoslovakia, and East Germany, tanks of the Czech and East German armies, and tanks in two armored divisions of the Polish army.

4. Stephan Geisenheyner, "A Defensive Weapons Mix for Europe: *Pandora, Medusa, Dragon Seed*," *Survival*, Vol. 13 (September 1971).

5. Trevor Cliffe, *Military Technology and the European Balance*, Adelphi Papers, 89 (London: International Institute for Strategic Studies, 1972), p. 20.

"tail" as possible in every theater, particularly in view of current manpower constraints. The problem, however, is not as clear-cut as some observers have suggested. A number of questions are related to the issue, none of which can be answered unequivocally. What is the presumed duration of the conflict? What manpower should be counted as support and what as combat? What are the consequences of a twenty-five-year-old U.S. peacetime deployment in Europe for a realistic war-fighting combat-to-support ratio? What is the effect of the demands on Army manpower by other Department of Defense commands and agencies operating in Europe? What is the optimum combat-to-support ratio?

In the aggregate, four and one-third U.S. divisions deployed in Europe field approximately 66,000 personnel. Units in Europe that are classified by the Army as division support contain an additional 89,000 men (six and two-thirds supporting increments). Another 44,000 men perform theater-wide special mission and general support functions, such as intelligence, transportation, communications, and logistics activities; command, control, and operation of tactical nuclear weapons; joint service activities; and maintenance of facilities supporting the peacetime deployment posture. The combat-to-support ratio of all U.S. ground forces in Europe (division manpower compared to the total deployment) is thus 66,000 to 133,000, or 33 percent combat and 67 percent support. If, however, one defines as combat the manpower in divisions *and* the combat elements in division support units (for example, corps artillery) *and* certain special mission units, such as missile forces, the ratio approximates 60 percent combat and 40 percent support.

Reinforcement scenarios usually call for the simultaneous deployment of a division and its Initial Supporting Increment (ISI), which together number about 32,000 men. For follow-up support of the division, a Sustaining Supporting Increment (SSI) of approximately 16,000 personnel can be deployed after about sixty days. Depending on *how* one evaluates the ratio of combat to support troops in these increments and *when* in the sequence one calculates the ratios, different perspectives emerge. At one extreme, if manpower in divisions is counted as combat and that in supporting increments as strictly support, the aggregate theoretical combat-to-support ratio for the first sixty days would be 50:50, and thereafter 33:67. On the other hand, many force planners claim that perhaps 30 percent of the manpower in all supporting increments have combat skills and would be used in combat roles (for example, rear area security forces, nondivisional armored cavalry and artillery units, and combat engineers). If these forces are accepted as combat formations, the resulting combat-to-support ratios become 65:35 and 53:47, respectively.

The issue of combat-to-support ratios therefore depends upon what forces are to be subsumed under each category. With respect to U.S. forces allocated to European contingencies, however, two important conclusions emerge from the foregoing discussion.

1. None of the combat-to-support ratios for U.S. forces calculated above is as favorable to combat as the 75:25 ratio estimated for Soviet ground forces. This asymmetry may be somewhat illusory since U.S. forces have qualitatively superior equipment, the maintenance of which requires a larger support "tail." Nevertheless, the difference is so great as to suggest widely differing assumptions about duration of conflict. Since greater support resources serve to increase the staying power of engaged forces, they constitute a hedge against the possibility of protracted conflict; fewer support forces increase initial combat capability, in part at the expense of capability for protracted conflict.

2. Relatively low *aggregate* combat-to-support ratios are in themselves no proof of an inefficient distribution of resources. It is necessary to examine the specific structures of support forces and to analyze carefully the relevance of their functions to a short-war contingency in Europe.

Tactical Air Forces

U.S. tactical fighter wings in Europe are located in England (three) and West Germany (four). Another tactical fighter wing is based at Torrejon, Spain; and a separate tactical fighter squadron is located in the Netherlands. Reconnaissance and airlift wings are split between British and West German bases. While British bases are more secure from air attack, their distance from the Central Front (350 to 400 miles) reduces their usefulness for combat purposes. Thus tactical aircraft in Great Britain would need to be refueled en route or transferred to operational bases in West Germany or one of the Benelux countries for efficient use in the Central Region. However, continental bases and particularly those in West Germany are more vulnerable to attack by Pact aircraft, and NATO has taken positive steps through the European Defense Improvement Program to improve its protection of those bases.

NATO-deployed U.S. Air Force fighter-attack aircraft number about

500. This force, when combined with allied forces in the Center, amounts to about 2,700 fighter-attack aircraft. The Pact's M-day total is about 5,500. All U.S. aircraft are first line—F-4s, F-111s, and A-7s—and have greater speed, longer range, and larger payload capacity than do most Pact aircraft. Nevertheless, to offset partially the Pact's numerical advantage, NATO depends primarily on reinforcements from both active and reserve formations in the United States. Asian deployments are also a potential source though they would probably be retained in Asia for possible contingencies in that area of the world.

All of these factors suggest that about 1,400 U.S. Air Force fighter-attack aircraft—in addition to those currently in Europe—could be deployed to the continent within thirty days: 500 from U.S.-based active wings, 600 from reserve units, approximately 150 from Asia/Pacific-based Air Force units, and about 120 from one Marine air wing associated with the NATO-oriented Marine division. The NATO total (aircraft deployed plus reinforcements) by M + 30 would thus amount to about 4,200; the Warsaw Pact during the same period could amass well over 6,000 tactical combat aircraft. (See Chapter 4, Table 4-1.)

Regardless of this quantitative shortfall, many observers believe that the central weakness of U.S. tactical air power available for European contingencies lies in its structure and mission orientation, neither of which is geared to the requirements of a short war. Prevailing U.S. tactical air doctrine holds that the overriding objective of the NATO air forces must be to establish dominance over the enemy in the air, not just over the immediate battle area but throughout the theater of operations. In view of the present strength of NATO air forces relative to those of the Warsaw Pact, winning total air supremacy may be an overambitious goal; at a minimum it would involve a time-consuming campaign that might not be completed in a short war. Moreover, preoccupation with the air battle appears antithetical to the requirements of a short war since it could well deny numerically inferior U.S. ground combat forces the direct-fire support that might prove decisive. Supremacy in the air would be worth little if, in the meantime, NATO forces had been defeated on the ground.

The relatively low priority that close air support receives under current doctrine is reflected in the structure of U.S. tactical air forces. The U.S. Air Force at present contains twenty-one operational tactical fighter wings. Only three are composed of aircraft that are optimally suited for the close support role (A-7s), and none of them are stationed in

Europe. The remaining eighteen wings are made up of expensive multipurpose planes (mostly F-4s and F-111s) that are designed primarily for achieving air superiority and for conducting a subsequent deep interdiction campaign, objectives of but marginal value in a short war in the Central Region.

CHAPTER FOUR

U.S. FORCES AND THE MILITARY BALANCE IN THE CENTRAL REGION

The foregoing assessments of the Warsaw Pact and NATO conventional military power in the Central Region suggest a number of conclusions with respect to both the general balance of forces in that area and the contribution of the United States to the region's forward defense. Many of these conclusions are not new; they have for years been the subject of considerable discussion. The same can be said of some of the authors' proposals—set forth in the chapters that follow—which are designed to achieve a new U.S. force posture. Yet despite a failure in the past to adopt these proposals, in the authors' opinion they make sense and should again be investigated, particularly at a time of intensifying debate over U.S. force levels in Europe and ongoing mutual and balanced force reductions (MBFR) negotiations with the Warsaw Pact countries.

1. The authors' first conclusion is that *the numerical balance of military forces in the Central Region is not unfavorable to the Atlantic Alliance.* Pact forces are clearly larger but, as may be seen in Table 4-1, at no stage during the crucial first sixty days of mobilization is the Pact likely to achieve a two-to-one superiority over NATO in total deployed military manpower, combat troops, or tactical aircraft. Only in tanks does the Pact have an overwhelming superiority. Yet without such an advantage in all of these key elements of military power the prospects for a quick and decisive Pact victory are highly unfavorable. Indeed, as was noted earlier, conventional wisdom holds that a three-to-one margin is the minimum required for a reasonable chance of success. Moreover, as was also noted earlier, the Pact's admittedly large numerical superiority in tanks and planes is offset somewhat by NATO's qualitative advantage in those weapons and by NATO's formidable anti-tank defenses.

On the other hand, it is important to recognize that the Pact's M day

Table 4-1. Comparison of Warsaw Pact and NATO Forces Available for Combat in the Central Region on M Day, M + 30, and M + 60[a]

Thousands

Force component	*M day*	*M + 30*	*M + 60*
Total deployed military manpower[b]			
Total Warsaw Pact[c]	576	1,076	1,241
USSR	339	677	842
Total NATO[d]	660	1,045	1,105
U.S.	200	285	345
Ground combat troops[b]			
Total Warsaw Pact[c]	432	807	931
USSR	254	502	632
Total NATO[d]	365	555	585
U.S.	90	130	160
Tanks[e]			
Total Warsaw Pact[c]	11.8	20.3	21.8
USSR	6.9	12.9	15.2
Total NATO[d]	6.7	7.7	8.2
U.S.	1.2	1.9	2.3
Tactical combat aircraft[f]			
Total Warsaw Pact[c]	5.5	6.7	8.4
USSR	3.7	4.9	6.6
Total NATO[d]	2.7	4.2	4.7
U.S.	0.6	2.0	2.5

Sources: Authors' calculations, based on data in International Institute for Strategic Studies, *The Military Balance 1972–1973* (London: IISS, 1972), pp. 7–13; T. N. Dupuy and Wendell Blanchard, *The Almanac of World Military Power*, 2d ed. (T. N. Dupuy Associates, 1972), pp. 133–52; "Reinforcements for Europe," *Strategic Survey* (London: IISS, 1973), pp. 19–23; and Irving Heymont and Melvin H. Rosen, "Five Foreign Army Reserve Systems," *Military Review*, Vol. 53 (March 1973).

a. General assumptions are that (1) hostilities are not initiated from M day through M + 60; (2) all Pact divisions located in East Germany, Poland, and Czechoslovakia that are near 100 percent strength are available for deployment opposite NATO Center on M day; (3) two Czech "cadre" divisions are available by M + 30; (4) only two Polish divisions are at full strength on M day, the rest being available by M + 7; and (5) no Category III divisions in the Soviet Army are available by M + 60.

b. Numbers of combat troops on both sides were estimated by applying the following combat–support ratios to deployed divisions: for non-U.S. NATO divisions, 65:35; for U.S. divisions, roughly 50:50; and for Eastern European and Soviet divisions, 75:25.

c. Warsaw Pact forces, as well as those of the USSR, are calculated on the basis of political assessments and readiness factors; they include the entire armies and air forces of East Germany, Poland, and Czechoslovakia. Forces from Hungary, Rumania, and Bulgaria do not appear in the table. For Soviet ground forces, post–M-day transfers of divisions to the Central Region from inside Russia are: twenty-four divisions by M + 30 and twelve more divisions by M + 60. The M-day strength of Soviet tactical air forces equals about one-half of the fighter aircraft assigned to the Tactical Air Force (TAF). By M + 60 are added one-third of the Air Defense Command's tactical aircraft plus another one-third of TAF aircraft and two-thirds of the aircraft assigned to the Air Defense Command.

d. NATO countries assumed to be contributing to the Central Front are Belgium, the Netherlands, Great Britain, Canada, West Germany, France, and the United States. Forces available on M day and through M + 60 are considered to be as follows: for non-U.S. NATO forces, all active divisions except for two in Britain, plus the equivalent of three divisions composed of combat units in the German Territorial Army available by M + 30. The buildup of U.S.-based divisions is assumed to be as follows: plus two and two-thirds by M + 30 and two more by M + 60 (including one Marine division). U.S. M-day aircraft would consist of 500 planes now in Europe plus 120 with the Sixth Fleet. Added by M + 30 would be 1,100 from the United States (active and reserve), 150 from U.S. deployments in Asia, and 120 assigned to one Marine air wing; by M + 60, 200 more aircraft are taken from U.S. reserve formations, 120 more from the active Air Force, and 120 from a second Marine air wing. Approximately 240 planes from four Atlantic Fleet carriers at M + 30 and 180 planes from three additional carriers at M + 60 have not been included, but could provide marginal additional air support in the Central Region.

e. Medium tanks only.

f. Does not include reconnaissance and transport aircraft or attack helicopters.

would probably (although not necessarily) precede NATO's by several days, since the decision to mobilize NATO's forces would in all likelihood be in response to the Pact's mobilization. Of course, the greater the time between the respective mobilizations, the less would be NATO's ability to sustain a not unfavorable force ratio vis-à-vis the Pact in the ensuing stages of mobilization; however, a delay of but a few days would not affect the balance decisively.[1] It is generally assumed, moreover, that any major Pact mobilization along the Central Front would soon be discovered and that NATO would respond quickly with appropriate countermeasures. For these reasons and for the sake of analytical simplicity, estimates in this study of comparative force buildups, unless otherwise specified, are based on the assumption of simultaneous mobilization.

The realization that NATO's conventional forces are not decisively outnumbered in the Central Region is not new, although it runs contrary to much informed opinion in both the United States and Western Europe.[2] Enthoven and Smith reached a similar conclusion several years ago in their comprehensive study, *How Much Is Enough?*[3] A more recent Department of Defense study concluded that eighty-five divisions and 5,000 to 6,000 tactical aircraft constituted the "designated [Pact] threat," that is, those forces believed certain to be available for a war in Central Europe.[4] While impressive, these numbers alone are not decisive.

Of notable concern, however, is the asymmetry of opposing force dispositions within the Central Region. Although the regional balance of forces may be satisfactory to the Atlantic Alliance, local force ratios along certain key sectors of the Central Front (particularly in the North German Plain) are potentially of decisive advantage to the Pact.

2. The second conclusion is that *the main weakness of NATO's conventional forces lies less in their smaller numbers than in their posture.* Al-

1. The effects of nonsimultaneous mobilization are discussed in Appendix C.

2. For example, in June 1973 NATO intelligence chief Admiral Gunter Poser, in a presentation before the alliance's Defense Planning Committee, claimed that Pact troops in Central Europe outnumbered U.S. and NATO troops in the same region 700,000 to 350,000. The figure for the U.S. and NATO troops is quite mystifying since the U.S. Army, Europe (USAREUR) and active West German ground forces alone at present number over 450,000 effectives. Kingsbury Smith, "NATO Troops Reported Outnumbered 2–1," Baltimore *News American,* June 20, 1973.

3. Alain C. Enthoven and K. Wayne Smith, *How Much Is Enough? Shaping the Defense Program 1961–1969* (Harper and Row, 1971).

4. Michael Getler, "Study Insists NATO Can Defend Itself," *Washington Post,* June 7, 1973.

though Soviet and Eastern European armies are deliberately and effectively designed for a short war, Western European and particularly U.S. forces, despite formal deference to the requirements of abbreviated conflict, are generally geared for a war of extended duration. NATO's so-called hedges against a long war are in fact so extensive that they inhibit the alliance's capability to fight a short war.

For Western European and especially U.S. ground forces, low ratios of combat to support troops, dependence on lengthy mobilization of undertrained reserves as a primary source of major reinforcement, and combat orientation of tactical air forces toward air superiority and deep interdiction at the expense of close support of ground forces are justifiable mainly as preparations for protracted conflict. Yet this is precisely the type of war that is least likely to occur in Europe because Soviet and Eastern European forces are structurally designed and doctrinally propelled toward a massive blitzkrieg, not a repeat of World War II. Indeed, by squeezing the maximum amount of combat power out of its available forces, the Pact has placed virtually all of its eggs in the short-war basket.

In sum, NATO has postured its forces to fight the wrong war and, in doing so, may have stripped itself of the capacity to wage the one it will probably have to face. The presumption of a short war as the most likely contingency in Europe does not, of course, preclude the need for hedges against a protracted one; in recent history the expectation of abbreviated conflict has often proved to be wrong. The important point, however, is that an inability to survive a short war makes preparations for a long one superfluous.

With respect specifically to U.S. forces committed to NATO, two sets of conclusions emerge from the analysis. The first set relates to present structural constraints on the ability of those forces to meet the requirements of a short war.

a. *The low ratio of combat to support troops within the 199,000-man U.S. Army, Europe (USAREUR) is unsuitable for a short war.* The allocation of more than one-half of all U.S. ground forces on the continent to logistics and other support functions greatly reduces the amount of combat power immediately available to USAREUR. Against a larger enemy, which musters three combat troops for each soldier in a supporting role and whose strategy calls for a brief conflict of great intensity, U.S. fighting forces, as presently configured, could well find themselves decisively outnumbered and outgunned on the battlefield during the crucial first few weeks of hostilities.

b. *The rate at which continental U.S. (CONUS)-based forces are deployable to Europe is too slow.* A cumbersome legacy of the Second World War, America's present structure of mobilization and deployment of active and reserve formations is not attuned to the realities of a short war. It is highly unlikely, for example, that the United States could augment its four and one-third divisions now in Europe by more than three and two-thirds additional divisions during the first thirty days of mobilization. The fact that the Soviet Union can more than double both its divisional and its nondivisional forces in Eastern Europe during the same period not only would place U.S. and NATO forces at a temporary disadvantage but also might serve to encourage, in an atmosphere of crisis, a preemptive attack by the Warsaw Pact.

c. *The primary mission orientation of U.S. tactical air forces toward the time-consuming acquisition of theater-level air superiority as a prerequisite to a deep interdiction campaign severely constricts the amount of air-delivered firepower available to engaged ground formations.* The Pact's vast quantity of both aircraft and airfields makes NATO's timely achievement of air superiority highly dubious. Moreover, NATO's devotion to superiority and interdiction requires investment in more expensive, and therefore fewer, aircraft. Yet a short, intense conflict argues for greater emphasis on close air support than it receives under present doctrine and aircraft design philosophy; without massive air support, an outnumbered U.S. ground force could conceivably be overwhelmed regardless of the ultimate outcome of the air battle.

The second set of conclusions relates to additional weaknesses that serve to inhibit the full realization of the overall combat effectiveness of U.S. forces in Europe, however those forces may be structured.

a. *Foremost among them is the fact that virtually all USAREUR combat formations are located astride less likely corridors for Warsaw Pact invasion.* The advantages of the North German Plain (and other areas north of current U.S. dispositions) over southern Germany as an axis of attack were discussed above; it is no coincidence that the bulk of Soviet military power forward-deployed in Eastern Europe is positioned opposite the former and not the latter. Moreover, the present locus of U.S. units risks their encirclement by a southward turn of westward-advancing Soviet forces.

b. *The vulnerability of existing U.S. lines of communication in Europe is another obvious weakness.* For example, the Bremerhaven line of communication (LOC), which constitutes the main channel of supply for the U.S. Seventh Army, is both unnecessarily long and imprudently close (at one point, less than ten miles from the East German border) to the Central Front. It could be severed with relative ease by advancing Pact forces, probably during the first few hours of combat; should this occur, U.S. forces might be forced to withdraw from their own logistics base.

c. *Equipment for overseas reinforcements prepositioned in Europe is concentrated, vulnerable, and difficult to maintain.* Unprotected vast stockpiles, which are located essentially in three major storage areas, are destabilizing, since during an East-West crisis and opposing force buildup, they would be a tempting target for Pact strikes. Permanent storage of large, congested equipment inventories also presents a major security problem and almost unmanageable maintenance difficulties.

d. *Tactical flexibility of U.S. and allied forces in the Center is limited by the policies and organizations of participating national commands.* Current basing arrangements and logistics support policies and organizations are for the most part national in character. Peacetime dispositions and support requirements of national governments are not optimally geared to combat needs. In wartime, they would inhibit the flexible and timely shifting of combat forces from one sector to another to influence the action at a decisive point. This capability is essential to overcoming the attacker's initiative.

CHAPTER FIVE

INCREASING THE AVAILABILITY OF U.S. GROUND FORCES FOR CONTINGENCIES IN NATO CENTER

The discussion above of Warsaw Pact and NATO military capabilities and force structures in the Central Region strongly suggests that the decisive phase of a major conflict there would be of relatively short duration. That is to say, if a successful defense by the NATO allies were achieved, the nature of the defense (well forward) would dictate an early outcome; however, if the defense were unsuccessful, the nature of the Warsaw Pact offensive thrust could assure a rapid advance and quick occupation of key objectives in the West. A stalemate resulting from either a successful NATO forward defense or a rapid Pact advance might result in a negotiated settlement or escalation to nuclear weapons.

It is also unlikely that mobilization and reinforcement would continue for long before a conflict would begin since the longer the buildup, the less favorable for the Pact would be the regional force ratio. Moreover, a long buildup period before an attack would strongly favor the defender by giving him time to prepare the battlefield. Certainly if the battle were joined as a result of accident or military miscalculation, activity before D day would be even more limited. The same holds true for a premeditated surprise attack by the Pact, although the forces the Pact could amass without detection would be relatively small.

The doctrine and organization of each national force committed to NATO Center should therefore be attuned to the requirements of a limited buildup in preparation for a short, intense conflict. This is true particularly for U.S. general purpose forces, which are to provide a major share of reinforcements for the Central Region. Specifically, (1) U.S. ground forces should be postured to contribute to a strong, conventional defense at the very outset of hostilities, and (2) U.S. tactical air forces should be structured to concentrate heavily on a successful initial defense of "battlefield" air space and on close support of engaged ground forces.

Improving Ground Force Deployments

The present U.S. ground force posture was shown in Table 3-2 above. The four and one-third divisions (with appropriate support) deployed forward in NATO Center are to be reinforced initially by about two-thirds of a continental United States (CONUS)-based division, which will deploy rapidly to prepositioned equipment in West Germany. Subsequent reinforcements are either to deploy to the points where the remaining stocks were prepositioned or bring equipment with them after more extended periods of preparation. Reserve combat forces are not expected to be available for deployment until near the end of or after a ninety-day period following M day. The present active-reserve structure for ground forces thus reveals a deployment concept that can best be described as a surge commitment followed by a long (and critical) lull in reinforcement. This condition is partially a function of the two basic division structures in the active and reserve components—active divisions with relatively high readiness, based on training, strength, and disposition, and reserve divisions in a very low state of readiness. It is also a legacy of history; since the nineteenth century the United States has met its wartime manpower needs by relying on the slow and deliberate mobilization and deployment of reservists. Although suited to the demands of a lengthy conflict, this posture would hardly meet the need for a rapid, emergency buildup in Europe.

In contrast, post–M-day Warsaw Pact buildups (see Table B-2 in Appendix B below) are expected to be progressive and steady under any circumstances since Soviet forces contain several categories of divisions with staggered readiness criteria (see Table B-1 in Appendix B below). If the advent of hostilities (D day) coincided with mobilization (M day) or followed it by up to two or three weeks, NATO's capacity to defend the Central Front would be seriously weakened in the face of a more formidable Pact buildup during the same period.

If NATO is to offset sufficiently the likely Warsaw Pact buildup, modifications in the structure of U.S. ground forces are in order. The modified force structure described below is geared to these requirements, derived from the analysis in Appendix C below. The key feature of the new structure is a more integrated active-reserve organization tailored to the need for a timely, progressive buildup in NATO Center after M day. It is designed to meet the requirements of the likely Pact buildup in the Central Region (see Table B-2 below), taking account of two possible non-U.S. NATO buildups (see Table A-1 below). Thus a requirements matrix was deduced parametrically for the number of U.S. divisions needed to redress the NATO shortfall in combat power at each stage of mobilization. (See Table C-1.) The resulting sequence of U.S. land force deployments to Europe that would achieve the force balance deemed necessary to deter or defend successfully against a Warsaw Pact attack is:

	M day	*M + 7*	*M + 15*	*M + 30*	*M + 60*	*M + 90*	*M + 120*
U.S. divisions required	4	6	7	11	13	14	18

An examination of Appendix C reveals three key aspects of this calculation. First, it was assumed that while the Pact would mobilize first, NATO intelligence activities and decision-making processes would preclude anything more than a short time lag in NATO mobilization behind that of the Pact.

Second, only buildups from M day on have been considered. D day—when the fighting actually breaks out—could, of course, occur at any time. The vagaries of combat are such, however, that it is difficult to predict the course of events after D day. Thus likely buildups from M day onward provide a reasonable and more predictable basis for force comparisons. If a force capable of providing conventional deterrence is to be structured, the opposition must be convinced that initiating hostilities at any point during these buildups is not likely to lead to military success. More specifically, if Pact military planners in assessing the force balance in Europe cannot guarantee better division ratios during the buildup than those specified for the conditions analyzed in Appendix C, they would probably not be able to predict a quick victory.

A third feature of the analysis is that since this study focuses on NATO, only cursory attention has been given to possible non-European contingencies. If emphasis were redirected to other worldwide contingencies, new strategic guidance could result in a change in priorities and in ground force structure and composition; but the methodology described in Appendix C would still be appropriate for an analysis of any new requirements.

To meet the M-day to M + 120 division requirements specified above, the authors have examined the present division structure of the U.S. Army and Marine Corps. The Marines are included since their use in sustained combat in NATO Center is believed vital to an adequate defense. Even though Marine forces are currently geared to contingencies on the flanks, their participation would not be inconsistent with either current strategic guidance, which places priority on European contingencies and does not anticipate simultaneous major contingencies elsewhere in the world, or with past use of the Corps in sustained combat roles inland (for example, in Korea and Vietnam).

Appendix C describes in detail how U.S. division requirements could be met. Six divisions of two brigades each (equivalent to about four full divisions) would be in place in Europe on M day. The remaining brigade of each division would be located, with its support, in the continental United States for rapid movement by air to join its parent division by M + 7 and thereby round out a six-division force. An additional six Army divisions and one Marine division would be available in the United States for deployment to meet all requirements through M + 60. Subsequent requirements would be met by the Marines' one reserve division (at M + 90) and four Army reserve component divisions (at M + 120).

The deployment of ground forces to Europe at such a pace calls for a major innovation in present U.S. ground force structure—assigning to each Army and Marine division, whether active or reserve, a mobilization designation based on readiness requirement. On the basis of the above deployment requirements and the assumptions for other contingencies, not all active divisions need be ready on M day. Since the object is to sustain a steady buildup over time, divisions need be ready only in time to fulfill their commitment to the theater when required. If divisions were designated by mobilization category, this requirement would be met. Each division's category designation would indicate its readiness for deployment in an emergency. The categories would differ in the degree of integration of active and reserve units within each division, which could largely determine the time required to make that division combat ready.

A Proposed U.S. Division Structure

The authors propose that U.S. ground forces be organized to contain five categories of divisions, with the last designed as a hedge against an

Table 5-1. Proposed Division Structure of U.S. Ground Forces

Service and type of division	*Category and readiness objective*			
	Category A, M day	*Category B, M + 7*	*Category C, M + 30*	*Category D, M + 90*
Army divisions				
Airborne	1	...	...	...
Airmobile	...	1	...	...
Armored	3	1	1	2
Infantry	...	2	1	2
Mechanized	4	...	1	2
Subtotal	8	4	3	6
Marine Corps divisions	2	...	1	1[a]
Total	10	4	4	7

a. Falls between Categories C and D at M + 60.

unusually protracted conflict. The division structure shown in Table 5-1 for four categories of divisions is recommended. The fifth category, which will be described below, is not included in the table since it would be a reserve cadre unit. The reserve Marine division (Category D) has a readiness objective of M + 60 instead of M + 90. The former objective is compatible with its current configuration and would not be changed.[1]

Category A divisions would contain only active forces ready on M day. They would have all their equipment and supplies on hand and be fully manned and at the peak of training. Depending on the requirement, they could be forward-deployed, or they could be based in the continental United States and available for immediate deployment.

Category B divisions would have a readiness objective of M + 7. To meet this objective, reserve companies could be integrated into active divisions by organizing each maneuver battalion in the division into one reserve and two active line companies. Other components of the present Army division organization—the cavalry squadron, all artillery battalions, the air defense battalion, and the engineer battalion—would

1. With respect to worldwide contingency requirements, the new ground forces' orientation could be as follows: to meet the NATO requirement, twelve active Army divisions, four Army National Guard, one active Marine, and one Marine reserve, for a total of eighteen divisions; a total of four divisions (two Army—active or reserve—and two active Marine) would be Asia oriented; two Army (active or reserve) divisions would be withheld to meet minor contingencies; and one active or reserve Army division would be retained as a strategic reserve.

also contain one reserve and two active line units. All remaining units (mostly support) would have fully active manning levels to assure the effective sustained operation of the division in garrison activities during peacetime. The complete division personnel structure would thus be about 85 percent active and 15 percent reserve.

The key to Category B division responsiveness lies in the relationship of active to reserve forces. Because of the vital need for quick reaction, proximity of the reserve units to their parent division would be necessary, and the reserve companies should be recruited from areas in close proximity to that division. A surplus of critical company skills would also have to be maintained; a reserve company strength of 150 percent would guarantee a division's ability to meet its M + 7 readiness objective in an emergency. The number of reservists with certain critical skills should be double the anticipated need in case some were absent, for personal or business reasons, at the time of mobilization. This would assure the availability, immediately after callup, of 100 percent of strength. Personnel in excess of 100 percent when reporting for mobilization could be placed in a division manpower pool to provide the division with a small reservoir of individual replacements. If reserve component companies could be manned by Army reserves rather than by state-controlled National Guardsmen, jurisdictional problems could be avoided. Thus within the division, the active chain of command from battalion commander through the division commander would exercise complete control over and total responsibility for the training, administration, personnel, logistics, and maintenance support of the reserve companies, subject to appropriately revised federal regulations governing Army reserves. To improve readiness, each reserve company might contain some active personnel (perhaps technicians) in such key positions as executive officer, company clerk, armorer, supply sergeant, and vehicle mechanic.

Category C divisions would be ready for deployment by M + 30, necessitating active-reserve integration at the brigade level. The division would be composed of two active brigades and one reserve. The division base would contain a mix of active and reserve units according to the status of brigades.[2] Thus about 70 percent of the division's personnel

2. The following units in the Army division base would be composed of approximately one-third reserve and two-thirds active personnel: air defense battalion, signal battalion, engineer battalion, cavalry squadron, medical battalion, supply and transport battalion, and maintenance battalion. Of the direct support

would be active and the remaining 30 percent reserve personnel. The division would be structured, however, to facilitate immediate deployment on an emergency basis as a two-brigade force, with followup by the reserve brigade and its support within thirty days. As in Category B formations, reserve component units in Category C divisions would be drawn from the Army Reserve and located in close proximity to the active division to facilitate command and control. The active Army division commander would be responsible for the training, administration, maintenance, and other support of his reserve brigade, which should reduce the need for some technicians that are normally in reserve units. Exchanges of officers and noncommissioned officers between active and reserve units within the division as well as frequent liaison visits would be customary. Moreover, most reserve company training could be conducted during normal scheduled drills, while reserve battalion and brigade unit training might be scheduled to coincide with division exercises. Integration of operating procedures and communications at higher levels would thus be increased.

Category D divisions would contain no active units and, with the exception of the Marine Reserve division, would be formed exclusively from the National Guard. The aim of units in this category would be to achieve readiness by M + 90, an objective the National Guard has not yet accomplished. Although Army Category D divisions would not have active subordinate units, substantial administrative, training, and other support would be required and could be provided by active organizations at higher headquarters, by advisers, and by technicians. In each continental Army region, headquarters have already been established in the new Army reorganization to support and supervise reserve components more closely. This effort, which could be directed specifically at Category D divisions, would be most productive in achieving high readiness and effective procedures for mobilization. The use of more civilian technicians with critical skills and increased advisory support under Army regional headquarters direction could also be contemplated. Providing more reserve component drills (with commensurately increased pay) to some reservists with critical skills who could devote extra time would be an additional enhancement.

---

battalions in division artillery, two would be active, and one would be reserve. The Marine division base (which excludes maneuver battalions) would have commensurate manning in its comparable divisional units.

Primary attention would have to be paid to the status of equipment in the National Guard divisions. All equipment should be on hand, and it should be as modern as is budgetarily feasible and compatible with equipment in active units. For the other Army Reserve component units that would round out the combat forces in the reserve structure (the number of separate brigades and battalions proposed in Table C-3) the same concentrated supervision and support could be required as for Category D divisions.

As a hedge against protracted war and to make efficient use of the large pool of Army reserve officers and senior enlisted men, a final category, the Reserve Cadre Division (RCD), is proposed. These divisions would represent reserve component organizations of the support structure and would be cadre training units, which were not initially considered to be a part of division forces. The RCD upon mobilization would receive inductees, conduct all training from basic combat to advanced unit training, organize maneuver battalions for combat, integrate combat support and combat service support units into the division base as units were made available from other mobilization activities, and be prepared to deploy overseas as an integral combat-ready division upon receipt of all equipment. If equipment for RCDs were stockpiled, then the only readiness constraint with respect to deployment would be the length of the training cycle and the time required to organize for combat (perhaps about eight months); otherwise, readiness would depend upon the time-consuming delivery of critical equipment from the production line.

The authors believe that the present thirteen reserve training divisions should be abolished, and an appropriate number of RCDs created to help achieve whatever strategic objectives are sought. Depending on the number created, the total post-mobilization training requirement for divisional maneuver battalions could be accomplished by these units, thus freeing most active personnel for other duties. The peacetime reserve strength of the RCD might number 2,000 to 2,500 men, including the required complement of officers and men in the top four enlisted grades for all divisional maneuver battalions and about half the officer and top four enlisted-grade strength in the division base.

To support combat operations of Army divisions, aggregations of special supporting units are needed. For planning purposes these units are known as Initial Supporting Increments (ISI) and Sustaining Supporting Increments (SSI). They are described briefly in Appendix C, and their number and role under the proposed alternative force posture are summarized in Table C-4 below. No additional analysis of these support forces is necessary; however, the postulated requirement for them and their size (16,000 personnel per supporting increment) must be taken into account in order to estimate differences in manpower and costs between current and proposed division forces.

The Advantages of Restructured Division Forces

The specific *advantages* of restructuring division forces by category of readiness are:

1. It would permit force planners to budget only for the necessary readiness level rather than to plan for more forces than strategic guidance requires. Some analysts claim that since current active divisions are manned at various levels of strength, the same economy and effectiveness is now realized. The authors believe, however, that the current levels of active Army division manning, reliant as they are on an influx of *individual* replacements drawn primarily from the ranks of the reserve components to reach full operating strength, are not optimally efficient. Moreover, current authorized manning levels are highly unsuited to the demands of a short war in Europe.

2. It would avoid the morale problems associated with the present system, which tends to fragment reserve units when they are called to active duty and subvert unit cohesion; "fillers" are randomly removed from closely knit reserve units to join active units with which they have had no prior association.

3. Reserve units integrated into active Army divisions would operate under the more positive command and control that are characteristic of active forces and would be more responsively supported by the extensive resources available in the active division. The result should be an increase in effectiveness of the reserves and a significantly higher level of readiness.

4. Optimum use of active Army units and individuals in support of counterpart reserve units would be achieved, thereby enhancing the "one army" concept. In the areas of staff planning, training, operations, and logistics, the two structures now tend to remain isolated from one another—almost like two separate armies. Effective unit integration would facilitate commonality.

5. The proposed structure should enhance civil-military relationships

in local communities as well as improve the Army's public image. Reserve recruiting activities of the active divisions to which reserve units would be assigned, active command responsibility for the supervision and training of some reserves, and joint active-reserve force projects to stimulate local civil-military rapport could offset the social isolation of the military, which some observers believe may be partly a result of the all-volunteer Army.[3]

6. The new structure would make possible the maintenance of fewer reserve units. National Guard divisions would be reduced from eight to six, and separate brigades and battalions would be drastically cut. (See Table C-3 below.) Smaller reserves should ease the reserve recruitment problem that has arisen in the all-volunteer environment.

7. The structure should also improve reserve morale. The reserve units that are assigned to active divisions according to division category would wear the division insignia and have a "sense of belonging" to a unit that probably had a long and distinguished history and would be charged with a major role in U.S. strategy. The higher quality of equipment issued to reserve units and the superior training they receive with their active parent units would further increase morale. In the event of mobilization, reserve units would not be broken up to provide individual fillers for active units but would remain intact to accomplish the mission for which they had trained *together*.

8. The structure is compatible with recent proposals for a ready, globally responsive corps force, light or heavy,[4] containing about three divisions. Appendix Table C-3 reveals that from the proposed U.S.-based, Europe-oriented forces, a combination of one Category A mechanized division and two of the six M-day brigades (armored and mechanized), together with their brigade support, operating with two Category C divisions (one armored and one mechanized division having M + 30 readiness but available for immediate deployment as two-brigade divisions) would be available to form a heavy corps force. The formation of such a corps force, however, would affect forces committed to NATO. A light corps force could be constituted from the airborne division (Category A), a Marine division (Category A), and the Category C Asia-oriented

3. See, for example, Morris Janowitz, "The Decline of the Mass Army," *Military Review,* Vol. 52 (February 1972), and Colonel Robert Gard, Jr., "The Military and American Society," *Foreign Affairs,* Vol. 49 (July 1971).

4. A light corps would consist of infantry, airborne, or Marine divisions with little heavy equipment. A heavy corps would consist of armored and mechanized units.

infantry division, which could also deploy immediately as a two-brigade force. Both the light and heavy corps described above could be deployed without mobilization.

The Disadvantages of Restructuring

The possible *disadvantages* associated with division forces restructured according to categories of readiness are:

1. A major mobilization order would be required to achieve full strength in some active divisions. Of the eighteen proposed active Army and Marine divisions, eight would have to be augmented by reserves to achieve deployment status as a complete division. Category B Army divisions would need about 15 percent reservists and Category C divisions about 30 percent. Under existing statutes an executive order for mobilization would be necessary to put these reservists on extended active duty. The need for rapid mobilization, particularly for Category B division reservists, would require a change in present reserve obligations and call-up procedures.

2. Some active divisions in the proposed structure would be less ready than existing active divisions. Not only would some portions of a division be in reserve status, but also some active elements within the division on occasion would probably have been diverted to training, maintenance, and other support of reserve units, thereby lessening slightly their own readiness. However, since the new division posture has attempted to correlate readiness with requirements, this disadvantage may not be as pronounced as it appears.

3. Commanders of integrated—active and reserve—units in the divisions would have increased responsibilities. The nature of the readiness requirement is such that all integrated units should be under the positive command and control of active commanders at higher levels. For commanders, the reserve status of some of their units thus means a higher personal profile in the local community, greater time spent in monitoring their reserve units, and more detailed planning to assure coordinated, responsive integration during mobilization.

In addition to substantive disadvantages, a significant reduction of reserve components also would probably create strong opposition from many senior reservists, who would see in unit reductions drastic cuts in manpower as well as a partial emasculation of grade structure, particularly in the higher officer and enlisted ranks. In their eyes, promotion prospects would be severely curtailed, especially in reserve units that were assigned to active divisions. Streamlining the reserve forces would undoubtedly affect the grade structure, but there is little reason to expect that promotion rates would be lowered further if efficient personnel management procedures and a "mobilization designation" policy were used. In reserve companies that are integrated with active Category B divisions, promotion potential could be limited to the rank of captain; however, within the division there is no reason not to designate for reservists certain positions requiring the rank of major or lieutenant colonel. These positions might include those of unit executive officers in some units, assistants or section chiefs on the division general staff, and perhaps G-5 or S-5 (Civil Affairs) officers in some divisional units. Enough positions could be designated for reservists to retain the promotion incentive. Only a small number of positions within the division need be set aside to accommodate the competitive selection of a few outstanding reservists for higher responsibility. In Category C divisions, the promotion potential for reservists would be adequate within the reserve brigade. Reserve Cadre Divisions, of course, would offer a broad potential for promotion to the highest ranks.

The proposed structural changes would also make a major reorganization of reserve components necessary, which would require congressional approval. Legislation proposing changes in reserve structure has traditionally met strong opposition from lawmakers. However, growing budgetary constraints and the manpower limitations of an all-volunteer Army will probably compel a more realistic reserve structure in any event.[5]

Implications for Strategy and Costs

The proposed new structure, coupled with the new scheme for reinforcing U.S. ground forces in Europe, has a number of implications for strategy and costs as well as for Army organization.

1. The M-day presence in Europe of six two-brigade divisions could influence U.S. political strategy in the event of a major European crisis. If each of the six divisions secured and maintained its absent brigade's prepositioned equipment while that brigade remained stationed in the United States but ready for rapid deployment, then only men and individual equipment to fill out the divisions would need to be deployed to Europe in the event of a crisis. Initial reinforcement of U.S. forces in

5. For an exposition of these and other issues relating to the reserves, see Martin Binkin, *U.S. Reserve Forces: The Problem of the Weekend Warrior* (Brookings Institution, 1974).

Europe could thus be accomplished in a very short time by airlift. Moreover, it would be politically less provocative to an opponent than would the deployment of major portions of divisions (and "flags"); in the early stages of a crisis, the arrival in Europe of one or more headquarters and units of division size could exacerbate political tensions at a delicate moment, whereas the movement of men to fill out divisions already in place in Europe would be less vexing.

2. The shift to a six-division structure in Europe would re-emphasize to its allies the resolve on the part of the United States to defend Europe. The significance that Europeans attach to the number of U.S. "division flags" on the continent is such that they would probably view six reduced-strength divisions in place as a better guarantee of the U.S. commitment than four and one-third fully manned divisions.

3. The new force structure, given the continuing primacy of Europe in U.S. military strategy, argues for greater emphasis on armored and mechanized forces. Appendix Table C-3 describes major units of the current and proposed structures by type. The composition and number of Army divisions is notably different;[6] this is shown in Table 5-2. For the Marine Corps, the proposed division structure would transfer one active Marine regiment to reserve status to accommodate the assignment of one active division to the M + 30 readiness category.

4. Changes in the composition of active and reserve ground force components and an additional one-third division set of prepositioned equipment would require an initial investment for the Army on the order of $725 million[7] if no use were made of equipment collected from units and headquarters that would be eliminated from the structure. However, if equipment from active Army units that were to be deactivated were transferred to new active units, and if the postulated decreases in reserve

6. The present maneuver battalion strength in the various types of Army divisions is as follows: armored division—six tank battalions, five mechanized infantry battalions; mechanized division—four tank battalions, six mechanized infantry battalions; infantry division—two tank battalions, eight infantry battalions; airmobile division—nine airmobile infantry battalions; and airborne division—nine airborne infantry battalions. The proposed new maneuver battalion strength in army divisions differs from the current posture only in the armored divisions. These divisions would be reorganized into ten maneuver battalions (six tank and four mechanized infantry).

7. This estimate is in fiscal year 1974 dollars and includes procurement, operating, and maintenance costs associated with initial investment. The figure does not cover accession, training, or initial change-of-station costs. Calculations are based on estimates in the fiscal 1972 Army Force Planning Cost Handbook, U.S. Department of the Army; cost of living indices were used to convert fiscal year 1972 dollars to fiscal 1974 dollars.

Table 5-2. Composition of Present and Proposed Active Army Divisions

Type of division	Division bases[a]	Brigade head-quarters (within divisions)	Maneuver battalions: Tank	Mecha-nized	Infantry	Air-mobile	Airborne
Present active Army components							
Armored	4	12	24	20	...	...	...
Mechanized	4	12	16	24	...	...	...
Infantry	3	9	6	...	24	...	...
Airborne	1	3	...	...	...	...	9
Airmobile	1	3	...	...	...	9	...
Total	13	39	46	44	24	9	9
Proposed active Army components[b]							
Armored	5	14	28	19	...	...	...
Mechanized	2	14	19	28	...	...	...
Infantry	3	8	6	...	21	...	...
Airborne	1	3	...	...	...	...	9
Airmobile	1	3	...	...	...	9	...
Total	15	42	53	47	21	9	9

a. An Army division base is a standardized organization containing the organic headquarters and combat and service support units of the division, which control and support its maneuver battalions. The division base contains 8,600 to 8,900 personnel, depending on division type.

b. Each Category A and B Army division in the new structure would have three active brigade headquarters with all maneuver battalion headquarters active (though some battalions in Category B divisions have reserves integrated at the company level). Category C divisions would have two active and one reserve brigade headquarters. Each of the reserve brigades would have three reserve battalions.

components released equipment for use by the reserve units that would be added, it is estimated that an initial investment of perhaps $600 million (primarily for active forces) would be required for new equipment to establish the proposed force. The largest initial investment costs (about $290 million) would be for creating the two additional active division bases. If less modern equipment available in the inventory were used to form these bases and appropriate units elsewhere in the total Army force structure were designated to form them, then the total initial investment cost of the new force might be reduced to perhaps $300 million.[8] The modifications in Marine Corps structure should not involve initial investment costs, since one Marine regiment would be dropped from the active force.

Increased initial investment costs are only part of the picture. Even though the new force would incur some early one-time costs, there would be an overall manpower reduction in both active and reserve

8. The current force structure contains twenty-one division force sets of equipment (excluding prepositioned stocks in Europe). The proposed new force structure also has twenty-one division sets even though the numbers of each division type are different. If equipment exchanges are maximized, the costs of new equipment unique to certain types of divisions could be reduced significantly.

forces under the new force posture that would mean substantial savings in annual operating costs.

5. Implicit in the new structure is the availability of enough air and sealift capabilities to meet the proposed reinforcement schedule for NATO Center. Appropriate air and sealift resources must be identified and earmarked, and alternative planning to accommodate all likely NATO contingencies must be undertaken. Mobilization procedures for all units involved should be tested periodically. The authors recognize the stringency of the readiness objective for both Category B and Category C divisions. But the possibility that the proposals may be considered infeasible by some should not prevent a thorough examination and objective testing of the suggested concepts. For this, the immediate formation of a "test" Category B division and a Category C division would be prudent. Concurrently, the Department of Defense and Congress should cooperate in devising legislation that assures a responsive active-reserve structure for integration and timely mobilization procedures. Equally critical is giving highest priority in U.S. force planning to the air and sealift mission for NATO reinforcement. The Air Force and Navy must plan, train for, and demonstrate under operational conditions the capacity to support the proposed reinforcement objectives. In sum, the deterrent value and war-fighting capability of the United States in NATO is linked critically to the efficacy of deployment planning and the achievement of reinforcement goals by *all* services operating in concert. The credibility of NATO strategy in the Center rests, in large measure, on the certainty of timely U.S. reinforcement. To generate enough forces to offset those of the Warsaw Pact is of little value if they cannot be deployed in time.

6. A major implication of the new ground force structure is the expected saving in manpower and associated costs. Calculations based on an assumption of 100 percent manning in all units reveal that the active Army Division Forces would realize a saving of approximately 12,000 personnel spaces in the new structure.[9] For fiscal year 1974, active

9. Using the full-strength planning factor of 16,000 personnel each in the three increments of the Division Force (division, ISI, and SSI), which are described in Appendix C, the following calculations can be made:

Current force: 13 divisions + 10 ISI + 4 SSI × 16,000 = 432,000.

Proposed force: 8 category A divisions × 16,000 + 4 category B divisions × 0.85 active strength × 16,000 + 3 category C divisions × 0.70 active strength × 16,000 + 8 category A ISI × 16,000 + 1 category A SSI × 16,000 + 4 category B ISI × 0.75 active strength × 16,000 + 1 category B SSI × 0.75 active strength × 16,000 = 420,000.

Army Division Forces around the world had a manning level of about 93 percent of authorized strength. At this level the manpower saving offered by the new structure would be about 11,000 spaces. Two other alternatives for the new structure that offer higher manning levels and better readiness than the current force, with little or no increase in personnel, are: (1) the proposed new structure could be manned at 95 percent of authorized strength for approximately the same manpower levels in Division Forces as in fiscal 1974 (402,000 personnel); or (2) all Category A divisions and associated supporting increments could be manned at 100 percent while all other units are manned at 90 percent of authorized strength, with a slight increase in fiscal 1974 manpower in Division Forces (402,000 to 405,000). Department of Defense sources have estimated that for every space eliminated in Army Division Forces, from 0.35 to 0.5 space can be eliminated in the "general support" and "trained individuals" categories, which provide personnel and support to the divisions. If the conservative figure (0.35) and the savings in Division Forces offered by the 93 percent manning level are used, an 11,000-space reduction in Division Forces would create a further reduction of about 3,900 spaces in the support base. Thus the proposed new structure in Division Forces alone, by conservative estimate, could reduce the current active Army total manpower levels by about 14,900 spaces.

Expected budgetary economies are also notable. If the per capita active Army annual operating cost is assumed to be $14,863,[10] the estimated annual operating cost saving that would result from the proposed reduction in manpower for the active Army would be $221.5 million in fiscal 1974 dollars.

As for the impact of the new structure on reserve component forces, if units are manned at the current level of 93 percent of authorized strength, the major units of the proposed reserve structure described in Appendix Table C-3 would require approximately 625,000 personnel.[11]

10. Binkin, in *U.S. Reserve Forces,* estimates that the per capita active Army military personnel costs were $9,428 (in fiscal 1974 dollars). In the fiscal 1974 Defense Department budget submission, operating and procurement costs for Army Program 2 were $1,541.2 million and $866.3 million, respectively. Given the active Army fiscal 1974 Program 2 end strength of 443,000 (the majority of which consists of Division Forces), the estimated per capita operating and procurement costs for personnel in Division Forces are $3,480 and $1,955 (in fiscal 1974 dollars), respectively. Hence, $9,428 + $3,480 + $1,955 = $14,863.

11. Based on (1) the following estimate for average strength of major reserve units: divisions, 16,000; separate brigades, 2,000; and separate battalions, 800; and

The total fiscal year 1974 authorization for reserve components was 660,000 personnel spaces. Thus a maximum estimated saving of 35,000 reserve component spaces is possible under the new structure.[12] On the assumption of an annual Army reserve component operating cost of $3,580 per capita,[13] the maximum saving in annual operating costs expected from the proposed reduction in reserve component spaces would be $125 million in fiscal 1974 dollars.

Proposed structural changes in the Marine Corps would reduce the three active Marine divisions to two Category A divisions and one Category C division, of which approximately two-thirds (two regiments and proportional division support) would be active and one-third reserve

---

(2) a planning factor of 16,000 per supporting increment (ISI and SSI), the following calculations can be made for the proposed reserve force:

Division and Other Major Units

Divisions: 6 category D divisions × 16,000 + 4 category B divisions × 0.15 reserve strength × 150 percent manning × 16,000 + 3 category C divisions × 0.30 reserve strength × 16,000 = 124,800.
11 separate brigades: 11 × 2,000 = 22,000.
60 separate battalions: 60 × 800 = 48,000.

Supporting Increments for Divisions (ISI, SSI)

4 category B ISIs × 0.25 reserve strength × 150 percent manning × 16,000 + 1 category B SSI × 0.25 reserve strength × 150 percent manning × 16,000 + 9 ISI × 16,000 + 19 SSI × 16,000 = 478,000.

The total proposed reserve force is thus 672,800. In consonance with the current reserve component manning level of 93 percent of authorized strength, the proposed force strength would be:

$$672{,}800 \times 0.93 = 625{,}000.$$

(An assumption of 2,000 per brigade presumes an austere configuration of combat battalions and headquarters only. For purposes of commitment, combat support and combat service support would be required from reserve component ISIs as necessary at the time and for the mission required.)

12. This is based on the assumption that reserve component forces will consist only of units in the Category B, C, and D divisions, in the eleven separate brigades, in the sixty separate battalions, and in the appropriate increments (ISI and SSI) supporting Category B, C, and D divisions. No other reserve component units are contemplated. If, however, Reserve Cadre Divisions are created as an added category, reserve personnel to man these skeleton divisions (estimated at 2,000 to 2,500 officers and noncommissioned officers per division) would eliminate some of the saving in space in proportion to the number of cadre divisions established.

13. According to the fiscal 1974 Department of Defense budget submission, Army Program 5 (reserve components) costs are $2,364.9 million. Given the fiscal 1974 Army reserve components end strength of 660,000 personnel, the estimated fiscal year 1974 per capita annual operating cost for reserves is $3,580.

(one regiment and its share of division support). The troops supporting the Category C division would also be at about two-thirds active strength since these troops would not need an earlier readiness objective than that of the division they support. Thus the new structure would permit the transfer of about 9,000 manpower spaces in the Corps from the active to the reserve forces.[14] Navy Department sources indicate that the average per capita annual operating cost of supporting an active Marine is about $8,000 more than for a Marine reservist. Hence, the yearly saving achieved in the new Marine Corps division structure would be approximately $72 million.

In sum, the maximum total savings expected to result from the adoption of the proposed structure for Army active and reserve forces and for the Marines could be about $418 million in fiscal 1974 dollars.

7. The new structure could also permit a reduction in Army forces now forward-deployed in NATO Center and a modest saving in associated annual costs. Six divisions of two brigades each, with appropriate supporting increments forward-deployed in the Central Region, would require approximately 144,000 personnel.[15] This figure represents the total initial requirement for Division Forces only and does not account for other Army forces stationed in Europe as Special Mission Forces (for example, the Berlin Brigade) or the Army contribution to other major headquarters and commands (for example, the Strategic Communications Command, Army Security Agency). These will be discussed below. The strength of Army Division Forces currently deployed

14. A Marine division has approximately 17,950 personnel. The troops supporting the division located on the West Coast (to be designated Category C) number about 9,200. One-third of the total is approximately 9,000.

15. Using the full-strength planning factor of 16,000 personnel for each division, ISI, and SSI, the following totals can be calculated for proposed Division Forces in Europe:

Divisions: 6 divisions $\times$ ⅔ strength $\times$ 16,000 $=$ 64,000.
ISI and SSI: 6 ISI $\times$ ⅔ strength $\times$ 16,000 $+$ 1 SSI $\times$ 16,000 $=$ 80,000.
64,000 $+$ 80,000 $=$ 144,000.

A division maintained at two-thirds strength is a division minus one brigade and its organic division support, which are based in the United States. Two-thirds strength for ISI means that two-thirds of the total supporting units *by type* are required in place in Europe. It does *not* mean that all ISI units in Europe are at two-thirds of authorized strength. The remaining one-third ISI equivalent would be stationed in the United States and moved to Europe to join major units of the ISI as CONUS-based brigades join their parent divisions. Consequently those individual units in Europe which make up two-thirds of the total division and ISI structure are assumed to be fully manned.

in Europe is about 155,000 personnel.[16] This figure represents an 87 percent overall manning level for those divisions and supporting increments now in the Central Region, which is rather low by readiness standards. Thus the proposed new level for Division Forces forward-deployed in the NATO Central Region is about 11,000 less than the current level. Moreover, it is anticipated that the new division and supporting increment posture would contain subordinate units at close to 100 percent strength. Only about two-thirds of each division and two-thirds of some kinds of units in the ISI would be in place initially, but they would be fully manned. This posture has significant training, administrative, and operating advantages over the current 87 percent manning level, since units maintained at below 90 percent strength in peacetime are compelled to reduce training in order to maintain administrative standards and perform garrison chores.

Annual cost savings from an 11,000-man reduction in Division Forces in NATO would be fairly small unless the personnel removed from forces in Europe were eliminated from the Army force structure entirely. This elimination, however, has been accounted for in the overall reduction to be achieved in the proposed new force structure and described above. The removal of 11,000 military personnel from Europe would save about $3 million in operating costs that are peculiar to Europe and $77 million in balance-of-payments costs.[17] The projected savings stemming from European force reductions apply only to Army personnel and dependents associated with Division Forces. There are additional Army forces and dependents, as well as personnel of other services, that might be cut in line with changes in U.S. strategy and requirements for NATO Center. These possible additional reductions are discussed in Chapter 8.

16. The total Army strength in Europe is about 199,000 men, of which 44,000 are assigned to Special Mission Forces and forces supporting other activities.

17. According to testimony in *Hearings Before the Special Subcommittee on North Atlantic Treaty Organization Commitments of the House Committee on Armed Services,* 92 Cong. 1, 2 sess. (1972), p. 12797, the fiscal year 1972 Army budget projected a possible saving of approximately $52 million if U.S. Army forces deployed in Western Europe were stationed in the continental United States. The difference would be approximately $57 million in fiscal 1974 dollars. If 11,000 military personnel were removed from NATO Center, this would reduce the number of Army personnel there by about 5.5 percent, with a total saving of about $3 million. From July 1971 to June 1973, the estimated spending by U.S. forces in West Germany (including personal expenditures, the preponderance of which was by Army personnel and their dependents) was $1.4 billion a year. A reduction of 11,000 Army personnel and a proportionate number of dependents (5,500) would reduce spending in West Germany by about 5.5 percent, or approximately $77 million.

Repositioning U.S. Troops in the Center

The availability of U.S. troops for a short war in NATO Center may be affected as much by their proximity to the likely areas of major combat as it is by their capacity for rapid reinforcement. The analysis in Chapter 2 and in Appendix D shows that U.S. and allied contingents are not optimally disposed astride the probable corridors of invasion and, at some points along the Central Front, are dangerously outnumbered by Pact forces. The disposition of U.S. forces (V and VII Corps) in CENTAG is particularly unsatisfactory since it risks envelopment of those forces by a southward turn of Soviet columns advancing across the North German Plain.

U.S. maldeployment in Germany has long been recognized, and proposals for repositioning U.S. forces in NATO Center have repeatedly been made. The failure to implement these proposals, however, does not mean they have no merit. Strong NATO deployments using stacked defenses on the expected avenues of attack, with economy-of-force operations in less critical areas, would seem a much more prudent alternative (see Table D-2 in Appendix D below) to present dispositions. The concept of forward defense could be retained but applied selectively. In the more remote and less vital areas of the Central Region (principally those south of the Fulda Gap and along the Czechoslovakian border) economy-of-force operations could trade relatively noncritical space for valuable time, while from the Fulda Gap northward across the North German Plain forces would be arranged in depth to stop an enemy well forward and deny him key objectives.

To achieve this goal the authors believe that a northward redisposition of forces, particularly U.S. forces, is necessary. A major objection to this has been that U.S. force redispositions would be costly and difficult because of the considerable investment in existing facilities and the size of the forces in place in V and VII Corps areas.[18] How then might there be a new deployment that would both strengthen defense capabil-

18. A major redisposition of U.S. forces northward might also be interpreted by the Soviets as a hostile or threatening move, given the concentration of their own forces in the North German Plain. Reassurances to the Pact that redisposition was aimed solely at enhancing NATO's defensive posture and did not entail the introduction of additional forces into the Central Region (as did the Pact invasion and subsequent occupation of Czechoslovakia in 1968) would serve to mitigate such apprehensions.

ities and alleviate the turmoil of a major redisposition and evacuation of costly facilities?

Specific elements of the proposed redeployment scheme, which are elaborated in Appendix D, include the following: (1) transferring the U.S. VII Corps from CENTAG to NORTHAG, (2) eliminating or curtailing large bases in some of the present areas of U.S. operation, (3) exchanging appropriate facilities with the Federal Republic of Germany or establishing joint basing arrangements that would facilitate the movement of the VII Corps to the North, and (4) compensating for reduced base facilities by rotating units of some U.S. Division Forces on a short, unaccompanied-tour basis.

The favorable impact of the VII Corps redisposition on the military balance in the crucial North German Plain is assessed in detail in Appendix D. The proposal for unit rotation is based on that transfer and on the plan for the forward deployment of six U.S. divisions of reduced strength in the Central Region, three of which would remain in the V Corps area in CENTAG. The removal of the VII Corps to the north would be accompanied by the negotiated transfer of old bases to West German or other allied forces. In its new corps zone in NORTHAG the VII Corps would reorganize its units to create three divisions (minus one brigade each) and corps support forces. All six forward-deployed divisions would be disposed with two brigades and most of the division base in Europe, while one brigade and its division support would be located in the continental United States for rapid deployment in an emergency.

Figure 5-1 shows the disposition of division elements if each division contained the proposed ten combat maneuver battalions. Permanently located in the Central Region would be two brigades of each division. One brigade (area A) would contain four battalions positioned to remain in place at permanent facilities, with enough division and corps support to sustain continuing operations. A second brigade (area B) would be postured to contain two battalions that would operate from austere facilities on a rotating basis. The brigade headquarters, with enough support from higher echelons, would remain in place to provide continuing administrative and combat service support; but the two maneuver battalions would remain forward-deployed for only a short period since they would rotate on a four-month cycle with the battalions deployed in CONUS under the control of the third brigade. As Figure 5-1 shows, the third brigade and a division rear echelon would con-

Figure 5-1. Proposed Disposition of U.S. Division Elements

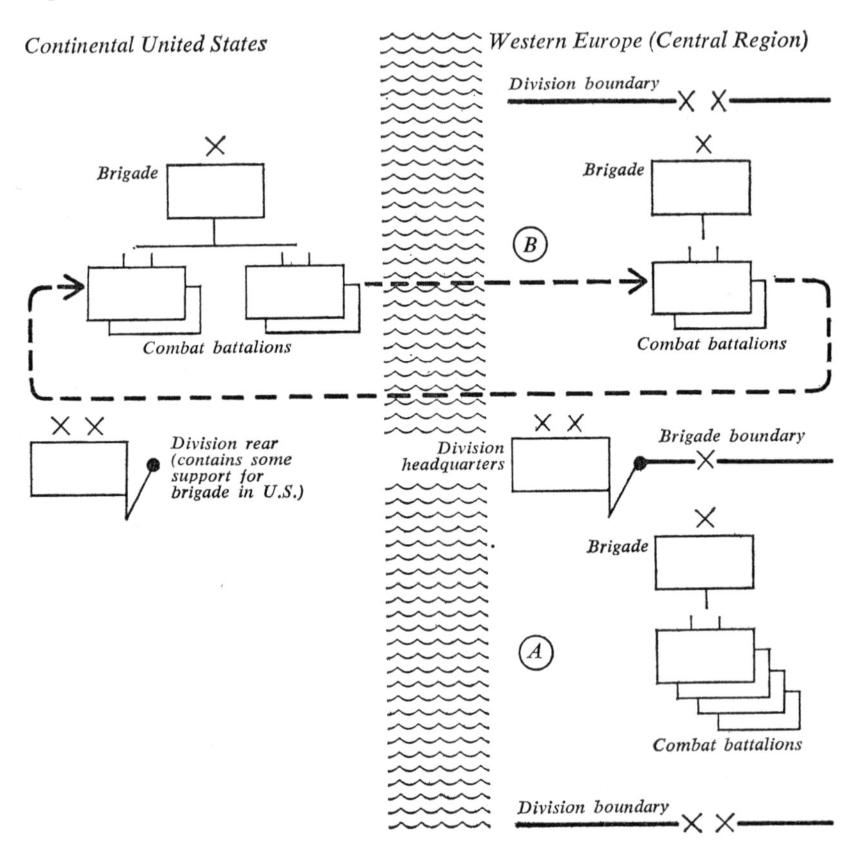

trol and support four battalions for rotation. This would permit the six battalions in the rotation cycle to spend four months in Europe and eight months in CONUS. At any one time, 60 percent of the combat maneuver battalions would be in place and operational. (About two-thirds of the total division structure, including headquarters and support, would be forward deployed.) The two battalions rotating to Europe would operate for four months on an intensive training and maintenance cycle with great emphasis given to field training. Austere facilities or joint basing arrangements in the new sector would reduce base operating requirements and costs.

Rotation would also facilitate better maintenance of the equipment prepositioned in Europe for designated divisional units located in CONUS. This equipment could be dispersed to appropriate locations in each division sector for ready access in the event of emergency deployment. Security and maintenance support for stored sets of equipment would be provided by the forward-deployed divisional units. As rotating battalions moved into their sector, they would use and maintain their own equipment while operational in the theater. Thus in a four-month period the rotating battalions would (1) remove their prepositioned equipment from temporary storage, (2) maintain it and train with it, and (3) conduct intensive maintenance prior to restorage. Frequent use and good maintenance practices should keep the prepositioned sets in better working order than is the case under the present system. The security and maintenance of small, well dispersed stockpiles by in-theater elements of the divisions also should permit more positive control and better command responsibility than under current prepositioning concepts.

The CONUS-based brigades and rear echelons of their respective divisions would also occupy permanent "homes" at installations in the United States. All dependents of the units that rotate to Europe for training and operations would be quartered and supported at the CONUS installation. Dependents of members of nonrotating units would be authorized in-country residence with their sponsors. Those in the rotating battalions on four-month "short" tours would be unaccompanied. The concept of division "homes" at specified posts in the United States would probably enhance volunteer Army recruiting and retention programs since the elements of stability and identification with a permanent locale in CONUS could be combined with periodic but brief tours overseas, where training would be both rewarding and productive, with some time off for recreation.

As for echelons above the division level, some corps support and command and control facilities should be retained in the various sectors of the Central Region, to be rounded out in the event of an emergency. Thus for about two-thirds of each forward-deployed division, the ISI that is part of that division "slice" should have about two-thirds of its required units forward. (These increments along with some SSI units could, however, be reduced further under a multinational logistics command, which will be described in Chapter 6.)[19]

19. In the late 1950s the Army adopted a policy of rotating units from CONUS to Europe. The results were not satisfactory, and the policy was dropped after several years. The authors' proposal would avoid many of the problems that plagued the earlier experiment because it does not encompass (1) the rotation of dependents, (2) the rotation of large units (divisions and regiments), and (3) the transfer of unit equipment between rotating units. The authors envisage a simpler and more austere policy.

The proposed concept for redisposing forces promises manpower savings for Army Division Forces in Europe of about 11,000; short-tour rotation would permit the return of a proportionately high share of Army dependents to the United States. Initial calculations suggest that about 31,000 fewer Division Force troops in Europe would be authorized to have dependents overseas. Based on a linear extrapolation this would lead to a proportionate Army dependent reduction of about 15.6 percent, or about 15,000 individuals, now living in approximately 6,000 authorized housing billets in West Germany, for whom about 6,000 housing units would have to be provided at or near appropriate installations in CONUS. Also, housing 15,000 dependents in the United States rather than in Europe would not reduce overall annual operating costs significantly. Moreover, if the 6,000 housing units required could not be found in CONUS at the appropriate locales, a maximum investment of $90 million to $100 million in military construction funds would be needed to build them, although it is unlikely that the entire requirement would have to be met by new construction. Quarters allowances paid if the 6,000 housing units were unavailable would amount to about $12 million annually.

Withdrawing 15,000 dependents from Europe would help to reduce foreign exchange expenditures. If one assumes an average annual expenditure of about $4,680 for each soldier *and* dependent in Europe, returning 15,000 dependents to the United States would reduce spending there by about $70 million a year.[20] On the same basis, and under the proposed plan for redispositions, withdrawing a total of 11,000 soldiers from Army Division Forces in West Germany and 15,000 Army dependents would reduce spending in Europe by about $121 million a year. This figure does not include savings that could be obtained from cuts in additional Army forces or in other services stationed in NATO Center—an issue to be discussed below.

Total savings in annual operating costs, achieved by using joint basing arrangements in new zones of operation, cannot be estimated. They would, of course, depend on the extent of such arrangements and on the disposition of U.S. forces that would facilitate joint basing. Savings could be substantial; for example, if one-third of U.S. Army forces now

20. It is estimated that the spending of U.S. Army forces and their dependents in West Germany, including personal spending, approximates $1.4 billion a year. The number of Army troops and dependents in West Germany is estimated at 299,000.

in Europe were located at bases operated jointly with the host country and that country funded 75 percent of only base operating support, the annual operating cost savings for USAREUR would be an estimated $150 million in fiscal year 1974 dollars.[21]

There would of course be annual costs associated with the rotation of units on a four-month, short-tour cycle. This expenditure would not be a new obligation, however, since the Army and Air Force at present conduct annual training exercises in rehearsal for rapid reinforcement of forward-deployed units in NATO Center. This operation, known as REFORGER, is designed to airlift elements of the 1st Infantry Division to Europe to pick up their prepositioned equipment and to participate in maneuvers with other U.S. units. Once they are in Europe, the cost of conducting training for REFORGER units would not be very different from the cost of extensive maneuvers conducted in CONUS. The Air Force, through its Military Airlift Command Industrial Fund, does charge the Army for the cost of round-trip airlift of troops and appropriate baggage. For example, the REFORGER exercise in fiscal 1974, which called for the round-trip airlift of about 11,000 troops, cost the Army about $6.9 million. Costs to the Air Force were about $0.3 million. The total amounted to about $655 per airlifted soldier.

The rotation of units in CONUS to their parent divisions in Europe every four months would approximate a REFORGER airlift exercise three times a year. If only the two maneuver battalions were moved at each exchange, about 2,000 troops per division would be involved, for a total of 36,000 troops a year (2,000 troops × 3 rotations × 6 divisions deployed), resulting in about $23.6 million annually in airlift costs. If, however, a wider scope were contemplated for the short-tour concept, then perhaps two battalions, plus a portion of divisional and nondivi-

21. The total obligational authority for base operating support (BOS) for the Army in fiscal 1973 was $2.4 billion. Base operating support is defined as support that provides to the military the equivalent of services that are normally provided in a civilian economy: maintenance of utilities, base supply activities, maintenance and repair of facilities, and standard-of-living maintenance (for example, provision of recreation, PX, and entertainment facilities). Thus the estimate that 75 percent of these costs are funded by the host country is but an illustrative one. The average Army strength during fiscal 1973 was 844,000, which means a per capita Army BOS cost of $2,840. In fiscal 1974 dollars this amount would be approximately $3,000. If the BOS costs for Europe are assumed to be roughly equivalent to the costs of BOS in the United States, and if one-third of USAREUR is assumed to be 66,500 personnel, then:

$$\$3{,}000 \times 66{,}500 \times 0.75 = \$150 \text{ million.}$$

sional units normally providing support during operations, might be airlifted for short tours. This might involve up to about 4,000 troops (combat and support) at each exchange for a total of 72,000 troops a year (4,000 troops × 3 rotations × 6 divisions deployed) and $47.2 million annually in airlift costs. But even this amount is not an exorbitant cost to pay for the suggested troop rotation concept, given the resulting benefits in tactical posture and the total saving it is expected to generate.

CHAPTER SIX

RECONFIGURING COMBAT SERVICE SUPPORT

Reconfiguring combat service support needs to meet the requirements of a short war argues strongly for (1) an increase in the ratio of combat to support troops in U.S. forces allocated to the defense of Europe, (2) the development of a multinational logistics command, (3) measures to reduce the vulnerability of prepositioned equipment, and (4) a major redirection of present USAREUR lines of communication in Europe.

Raising the Ratio of Combat to Support Troops

The analysis in Chapter 3 above concluded that the present ratio of combat to support troops in U.S. forces oriented toward NATO Center is clearly unsuited to the requirements of a short war in Europe. A subject of considerable controversy,[1] the low "teeth-to-tail" ratio in those forces represents more a preparation for a classic buildup and sustained engagement, "World War II style," than it does a structure designed to fight a sharp, brief conflict. If strategic planners really believed in the short, intense war assumption, it is highly unlikely that they would propose the current organization for support.

U.S. forces should be geared to the requirements of such a war and at the same time be prepared for a possible protracted conflict. Long-war hedges should be provided in force structure, logistics, mobility forces, and mobilization concepts. The list of specific adjustments in each area is long, and no attempt is made to discuss all of them in this study. It is

1. See, for example, Alain C. Enthoven and K. Wayne Smith, *How Much Is Enough? Shaping the Defense Program 1961–1969* (Harper and Row, 1971), Chap. 4; and Stephen Canby, *NATO Military Policy: Obtaining Conventional Comparability with the Warsaw Pact,* R-1088-ARPA (RAND Corporation, 1973).

important, however, to consider the areas collectively and systematically in planning for a higher ratio of combat to support forces. Land force structural hedges against a protracted war can be accommodated in part by the proposed categorization of divisions. Logistics guidance in the Department of Defense, which provides for high usage rates for forces in NATO Center, contains a built-in hedge since intense combat in all areas every day is highly improbable; thus rationing of some supplies and use at normal rates would conserve resources to meet later needs. Mobility forces must have a residual capacity for sustained operations over long distances. Mobilization planners must decide what is the appropriate industrial base for a protracted war, including the proper tradeoff between short-war stockpiles and industrial preparedness for a longer conflict.

Specific measures that would serve to improve the ratio of combat to support forces by reducing the number of support personnel in operational units include:

- *Increasing the number of small stockpiles in areas well forward and easily secured by troops in place.* The administration and disposition of the stockpiles could be handled by divisions or by an increase in the scope of activities of units in the Initial Supporting Increments (ISI) and a reduction in the requirement for Sustaining Supporting Increments (SSI). Specifically contemplated are a longer-term supply of rations and ammunition carried at lower levels and larger authorized stocks of repair parts. As a consequence, however, more effective use of modern containerization techniques and decentralization of transport resources to lower levels must be investigated.
- *Increasing "short war" reliance on the mobilization of civilian assets to operate the lines of communication and on the local economy for some logistics resources.* Diesel fuel, for example, is in relatively abundant supply in the local economy, and most military engines operate on diesel fuel. "Plugging into" local transportation networks and planning for the use of local stocks would not only reduce the need for support troops but would also facilitate the formation of a multinational logistics command.
- *Expanding the Army's use of nonstop "throughput" of supplies from ports to forward areas.* This new technique should be examined further for possible wider implementation. Unique organizational structures, transportation, and handling techniques should be conceived and introduced in order to eliminate major needs for supporting increments.

- *Adopting the unit replacement system.* Present reliance on the individual replacement system requires allocating large numbers of personnel to in-theater reception and assigning each incoming individual to his particular unit. Under the unit system, entire units could move directly to division holding areas from points in the United States, thus permitting a more rapid transfer of larger numbers of men and requiring fewer personnel to process them.
- *Reducing the in-theater requirement for extensive medical facilities and support.* For an intense conventional phase of conflict that is perceived as lasting only a few months at most, a policy of very early evacuation of casualties should be contemplated. An evacuation policy of one or two weeks[2] creates a large need for transportation out of the theater but significantly reduces the in-theater requirement for extensive medical facilities and support. The fact that return space on air transportation from the United States to Europe would be plentiful makes a very early evacuation policy feasible. However, one aspect that must be considered is the effect such a policy would have on the need for replacements. More replacements would be required, and the impact on the respective replacement systems (individual versus unit) would have to be carefully weighed.
- *Reducing resources devoted to the repair and evacuation of combat-damaged equipment.* In a short war extensive repairs and/or evacuation of combat-damaged equipment is of marginal importance and creates unnecessary burdens on the maintenance support establishment. A policy of abandoning or destroying inoperable equipment that cannot easily and rapidly be repaired should therefore be considered. It would be necessary to compensate for losses by increasing equipment stocks and maintenance floats (spares) in order to ensure that replacements would be available to meet the higher attrition rates expected in an abbreviated conflict.

These recommendations are but a small sample of the many modifications in support forces that might improve the ratio of U.S. combat forces to support forces. Furthermore, the authors make no attempt to evaluate the savings in manpower or costs that might result from the adoption of such measures. A cost analysis should be part of a detailed review of the total spectrum of support policies and operations designed

2. An evacuation policy of two weeks is one in which all ill or wounded persons who cannot be returned to duty within two weeks must be evacuated from the theater for further treatment.

to isolate and study the many organizations and functions that could be altered effectively in consonance with a brief but intense conflict in NATO Center.

The Need for a Multinational Logistics Command

If a short war is assumed, another measure that would serve to reduce the support establishment would be to organize a multinational logistics command (MLC). An MLC would also improve substantially the war-fighting capability of the NATO alliance, as well as reduce peacetime costs to all participants. The authors envision the formation in the Central Region of an operational support command, which would be under the direction of the commander of the Allied Forces Central Europe (AFCENT) and on the same level as the Northern Army Group (NORTHAG) and the Central Army Group (CENTAG). The command would be similar in organization and function to the U.S. Army's Theater Army Support Command (TASCOM).[3]

If this proposal were adopted, the commander of AFCENT would organize, command, and administer a support organization composed of forces contributed by all nations participating in the defense of the Central Region. He would exercise authority in both peacetime and wartime in the areas of supply and transportation. However, his authority over all procurement policy and operations in peacetime might be qualified because of economic considerations. Subordinate to him would be a commander of an MLC who would be on the same level as the commanders of NORTHAG and CENTAG. The responsibilities of the MLC commander would be to assure uniform support for all national forces operating in NORTHAG and CENTAG, to establish logistics policy, conduct detailed logistics planning, assign missions and allocate resources to multinational support forces under his control, and to set priorities for support. His area of operation would be the zone extending from the rear of each national corps boundary throughout the entire rear area, including the airheads and ports of entry into the Central Region. For most resupply, the unilateral logistics support responsibility of each national force would be limited to that within its own corps, and the interface with the MLC would take place at depots and facilities to which national forces would go for support.

3. See Department of the Army, Field Manual 54-7, *The Theater Army Support Command* (Headquarters, Department of the Army, March 1972), for a description of the organization, mission, and function of TASCOM.

Specific missions of the MLC would be the general support of national corps, direct and general support of multinational forces in the rear areas, and rear area security. The command might be organized along multinational lines in the fields of transportation, logistics support, area security, and engineering support. Personnel and medical support functions, which are uniquely national in character, could be performed by national forces under the overall supervision of the MLC commander.

A subordinate multinational transportation command would recommend policy for the allocation of transportation assets, manage intraregional military transportation systems, and coordinate the utilization of civilian networks and interregional operations. A subordinate multinational supply command would manage the receipt, storage, and distribution of supplies. This would include the requisitioning of common items, general depot operations, managing the maintenance of common equipment, and controlling indigenous labor service support. Although the procurement of some common items could be delegated to the MLC, procurement responsibility for major items could remain a unilateral national responsibility, with requisitions being submitted by the various national commands. Once they were procured, however, these items would enter the MLC supply and transportation system to be distributed to the unit in need. Thus logistics operations for items of supply unique to each national force would be integrated into the system to assure effective support in both peacetime and wartime. A subordinate multinational engineering command would plan, design, and supervise the construction or rehabilitation of ports, roads, rail networks, depots, airfields, missile and air defense emplacements, and other facilities. Technical engineering assistance to forces in the region and, where appropriate, real estate management also would be provided.

A number of important benefits would come from a multinational logistics command. First, the forces participating would receive more effective support without a commensurate increase in manpower requirements. In fact, some reduction in support manpower is to be expected. For U.S. forces oriented to NATO, participation in an MLC would mean that forces deployed in Europe could be reduced as a result of the proposed force structure modifications without any impairment of combat power. As reinforcing units arrived in the theater, the presence of an operational MLC would allow their combat-to-support manpower ratio to be improved substantially. For example, the normal division slice in a theater, made up of the division itself and supporting increments in the corps and field Army areas, numbers about 48,000 personnel. Of this figure about 16,000 are considered division troops. Another 16,000 men per division would probably be located in the corps area to provide combat and logistics support to the division. Approximately 16,000 more per division would be located behind the corps in the field Army and theater areas to provide logistics and combat support to forces in the corps. If the U.S. troops reinforcing Europe contributed to an MLC that supported U.S. corps operations, then the 16,000 men per division normally operating behind a corps to provide sustaining support could probably be reduced by at least one-half.[4] Thus a reinforcing division slice for Europe would require no more than 40,000 personnel. This configuration would significantly improve the combat-to-support ratio in that theater during a buildup and reduce manpower requirements (primarily in the reserves) for NATO contingencies.

If the Sustaining Supporting Increments in the reserve components were reduced by 8,000 each for the twelve active Army divisions and four Army reserve component divisions oriented to NATO Center in the new proposed posture (see Appendix C, Table C-3), an additional saving of 119,000 reserve spaces would accrue, with a consequent reduction in annual operating costs (in fiscal year 1974 dollars) of about $426 million.[5]

Second, if a multinational logistics command were organized, the joint basing of national forces, particularly at depots and installations to the rear of national corps, would be facilitated. The consolidation of personnel, facilities, and services could be readily and economically achieved, with beneficial results for the United States since joint basing agreements could partially offset the cost of maintaining U.S. forces in NATO Center. If European allies were willing to assume more of the expense for U.S. deployments in NATO, then joint tenant agreements at military installations on the continent would permit Europeans to assume a major share of the indirect or overhead costs of U.S. forces stationed

4. The authors' estimate is based on a perusal of the requirements for combat and logistics support at the field Army and theater level and an approximation of the contribution to an MLC that would perform the same functions in the transportation, supply, engineering support, and security areas. Unilateral personnel and medical support is assumed.

5. Based on an estimated per capita reserve annual operating cost of $3,580 in fiscal 1974 dollars and the assumption of 93 percent manning for the designated spaces saved in the reserve component units.

at joint bases. Since their own forces would operate from those bases as well, and since the facilities and civilian labor force would be largely local in character, it would probably be more palatable politically to those allied nations involved to assume a larger share of expenses. It should be noted also that joint basing arrangements need not be limited to support installations; any training facilities or other bases that are appropriate for joint tenancy should be examined for possible use.

Third, an MLC would increase the tactical flexibility and mobility of allied forces in the Center under wartime conditions. Senior military commanders and observers of the European military scene recognize the lack of flexibility in current force dispositions, which promise in wartime to generate difficulties in adjusting allied deployments to opposing tactical moves. The present national character of logistics support and restraints on multilateral resource allocation in an emergency severely inhibit the ability of the senior field commanders in the Central Region to shift national forces and reorient lines of communication in reaction to an attack. Multinationalization of the logistics effort would infuse tactical mobility and adaptability into the support base for allied forces and, in so doing, would improve the military balance in the Center.

If an MLC were created, both inertia and real problems would have to be overcome. Notwithstanding its superior tactical value and efficiency, proposals to move toward an MLC would continue to encounter, as they have in the past, stiff bureaucratic resistance on the part of national military establishments. The lack of standardized weapons and equipment serves as an impediment to multilateral logistics management. Moreover, common weapons development and procurement have not often been successful, although systems continue to be developed and produced as joint ventures.[6]

These obstacles, however, cannot hide the disparity of logistics systems and policies among NATO allies. Even stockage requirements are viewed in different perspectives; for example, U.S. forces maintain a resupply capability on the continent that for some items is as much as three times greater than the amounts stocked by European allies. But the rudiments of multinational coordination in the logistics field are present

6. For example, now in progress are the production of the HAWK surface-to-air missile, the ATLANTIQUE maritime patrol aircraft, the advanced swing-wing multirole combat aircraft (MRCA), and new field howitzers, as well as a joint European study of a new main battle tank.

in several NATO agencies;[7] and an environment of successful cooperation engendered by them could spill over into the operational support of commands in the field if the Supreme Allied Commander, Europe (SACEUR), backed by NATO's Military Committee, will plan for and request the North Atlantic Council to authorize the organization and full operational use of an MLC in the NATO Central Region.

Upgrading the Protection, Control, and Maintenance of Prepositioned Equipment

As currently disposed, prepositioned equipment for use by early U.S. reinforcements in the Center offers one of the most tempting targets for enemy attention in the entire NATO area, and it is highly probable that the giant exposed storage sites would attract substantial Pact resources aimed at their destruction in the early hours of conflict. The protection of prepositioned equipment would be extremely important in a short war since the first incoming U.S. reinforcements would be completely dependent upon it.

A successful initial strike against the depots could deprive the United States of at least 35 percent of its combat capability early in any buildup if they were attacked before reinforcements arrived from the United States. Indeed, the vulnerability of prepositioned equipment could well encourage a surprise attack, if hostilities were deemed inevitable, since such a tactical blow could outweigh any perceived disadvantage of attacking with minimum preparation. The depots are vulnerable to air attack, surface-to-surface missile fire, airborne assault, and sabotage. Although Pact elements attacking the depots would be subject to intense countermeasures and would probably suffer severe losses, a successful attack might be worth the price in the event of hostilities. For instance, an ideal mission for Soviet airborne forces, even at the expense of substantial losses, would be to assault and destroy prepositioned equipment.

7. Representative agencies are: the Central Europe Pipeline System (CEPS) for multinational supervision of the operation and maintenance of the integrated military pipeline system in NATO Center; the NATO HAWK Production and Logistics Organization (NHPLO), which, in addition to supervising HAWK missile production, provides the logistics support of HAWK units in Europe; and the NATO Maintenance and Supply Organization (NAMSO) for supply management of parts and logistics for several jointly used items of equipment.

Two further problems inherent in the current disposition of prepositioned equipment are those of accountability and maintainability. The magnitude of these difficulties surfaced in a recent report made public by the General Accounting Office.[8] The GAO revealed that a July 1971 Army Audit Agency report cited "errors in excess of $32 million in accounting for some prepositioned equipment" and that as of March 1972, accountability control had not been recovered.[9] The report also revealed that at the GAO's request an Army inspection team had checked about seventy vehicles selected from prepositioned stocks to ascertain combat readiness. The vehicles represented about 20 percent of the types stored. Of the equipment inspected, 76 percent was found to be unready for combat. The GAO report concluded that an estimated $64 million worth of repairs and replacements was needed to restore the readiness of all prepositioned equipment. Since the GAO report was presented to the Army significant steps have been taken to correct the problems. However, because of the current disposition of prepositioned stocks that require the services of over fifteen hundred personnel in equipment maintenance groups, abuses of policy and breakdowns of control can still readily occur.

An alternative to the present disposition would be to disperse prepositioned equipment to the operational areas of each of the proposed six forward-deployed divisions. The six-division force would be configured so that the two brigades of each division in Europe would secure the prepositioned equipment of the division's third brigade, which would be stationed in the continental United States. Supply and maintenance units of the division base would be augmented to fulfill the requirements of accountability and maintainability with respect to the stockpiled equipment. Thus the large number of personnel in equipment maintenance groups that now service the prepositioned stocks could be reduced to small augmentation teams in each division. Command responsibility for control would rest with the division commanders, whose own units in the United States would draw the equipment after airlift to NATO Center. The nature of this relationship should assure greater security and better maintenance than are now given the stocks. Under this alternative, prepositioned equipment would be dispersed well for-

8. Michael Getler, "GAO Finds Arms for GI Airlift Not Combat Ready," *Washington Post,* March 13, 1973.

9. Ibid.

ward, readily accessible, and controlled by the individuals and units that are dependent on its availability.

Two drawbacks are apparent in the proposed scheme of dispersal. Climate-controlled shelters and other semipermanent facilities have already been constructed at the present sites for the proper storage of certain weather-sensitive items. Most of these facilities could not be moved to new sites. Moreover, because of the need for a forward-deployed division to secure and maintain equipment for its third brigade, extra division personnel would probably be required, and time would be diverted from normal training and administrative activities.

As for the first drawback, it is known that the construction of many protective shelters is far from complete. The work that remains could be diverted to new sites in division areas, and sites already completed could be turned over to West German forces in exchange for some negotiated remuneration. By making use of smaller stockpiles that are under the control of divisions which depend on the operability of that equipment and are already using land and buildings that could store the stockpiles, dispersal would also reduce the considerable expense associated with operating the gigantic depots for prepositioned stocks, providing personnel to administer them, and absorbing the costs of associated inefficiencies, such as those detailed in the GAO report. The prospect of some offsetting reductions in facilities, personnel, and maintenance costs is therefore a real one.

As for the second drawback, training schedules and maintenance policies and practices of divisions in charge of the prepositioned stocks admittedly would have to be adjusted to provide more time for the security and care of the added equipment; but if these changes were properly planned, overall unit training and administration should not suffer significantly. Indeed, the tradeoff should reflect greater equipment availability and better unit readiness for any buildup in Europe.

For the prepositioned equipment destined for use by "dual based" support units that are required to service the divisions, joint basing arrangements in areas to the rear of forward divisions might create opportunities for the use of supervised indigenous labor and services to secure and maintain stockpiles. Some associated costs might be borne by the host government, in accordance with the joint basing proposal described above, in order to help offset the operating costs of U.S. forces in NATO Center.

Redirecting Lines of Communication

Secure lines of communication are important in any combat environment. However, a short war in Europe might not permit NATO to shift from reliance on its present vulnerable line of communication (LOC) to a more secure one in time to affect significantly the outcome of the conflict.

This study is one of many which have concluded that the current major LOC for U.S. forces in the Central Region (the Bremerhaven LOC) is an extended, tenuous logistics link, which for long stretches parallels the boundary between opposing forces and at some points is perilously close to the East German border. Its proximity to the probable initial points of contact when hostilities begin suggests that the LOC would be severed within hours of an attack. Even if it were not cut by ground troops, Warsaw Pact air and artillery forces could effectively interdict it, and then a major effort would be needed to redirect the line or to switch to air delivery under extreme pressure. Moreover, supplies moved by military convoy or rail along the 250-mile route not only require more transportation resources operating over longer periods than would a more direct LOC, but also must compete with nonmilitary imports for processing through one of West Germany's few major Atlantic ports. Finally the Bremerhaven LOC traverses the forward areas of the Northern Army Group, which contains the major corps forces of four other national commands.[10] Current NATO doctrine places responsibility for logistics support unilaterally on each national command.[11] The result is redundancy in logistics structures and competition for the use of lines of communication, which further reduce the flexibility and mobility of U.S. resupply operations and increase the cost of logistics support for all national forces.

To overcome the disadvantages of the present U.S. line of communication in Europe, the authors propose that a major redirection of the

10. The Netherlands, West Germany, the United Kingdom, and Belgium.

11. NATO organizational and administrative policy specifies that logistics is a national responsibility. Some authority is also given in wartime to SACEUR to redistribute assets among forces under his command, as required. There is little evidence, however, that current operational arrangements and announced policy have prompted detailed contingency planning for multinational logistics cooperation.

logistics network be undertaken. The proposal is not novel and has foundered in the past on various political and financial obstacles. However, it should be reexamined in the light of the overall change in NATO dispositions proposed in this paper.

Although the United States does not intend to use the Bremerhaven LOC during wartime but plans instead to relocate the LOC through ports in France or the Benelux countries, no specific funds, personnel, or facilities have been allocated for the purpose. Moreover, negotiations in that direction between the United States and host countries have not progressed much beyond the signing of pro forma agreements. The authors believe that at least partial operation of a Benelux LOC should be initiated as a hedge against unexpected hostilities. To redirect the present LOC "under fire" without some prior implementation of existing plans could seriously jeopardize a sufficient and sustained support operation during the critical early days of conflict. Operations along the Bremerhaven LOC could be eliminated in time or at least curtailed, as increasing reliance was placed on the new Benelux LOC.

Reorienting the logistics network to the Benelux countries would provide a shorter and more flexible LOC through a larger number of ports and would facilitate wider use of joint basing arrangements. It would also reorient logistics support behind U.S. combat forces rather than on their flank. A Benelux LOC would create a broader network of roads for the rapid movement of East-West traffic and would permit the use of additional major port facilities (for example, Antwerp, Rotterdam, and Amsterdam) for discharging cargo efficiently. To assure the dispersal of debarkation points and relieve congestion at major ports, a reorientation of the LOC would facilitate the use of over-the-beach operations along the Benelux littoral. If these proposals were carried out now at least in part, an efficient and rapid transition could be made in wartime if major ports were closed, and the flexibility of logistics support would be increased.

CHAPTER SEVEN

SHORT WAR IMPLICATIONS FOR U.S. TACTICAL AIR FORCES

Although this paper is concerned primarily with ground force requirements, some of the questions about tactical air forces raised by the short war concept should be mentioned, primarily as a guide to further study.

Planning for a very intense, but brief, conventional defense of Europe rather than a protracted one strongly suggests that U.S. tactical air forces should be oriented toward providing a greater amount of immediate support for engaged land forces than that envisaged in current U.S. tactical air doctrine and aircraft design criteria. This means more than merely assigning a different mission to existing aircraft. Also needed are new aircraft designed specifically for close air support. U.S. Army attack helicopters, such as the Cobra and the proposed Advanced Attack Helicopter (AAH), are of some value in that role, particularly in providing responsive, direct aerial fire support to front line commanders, but they are no substitute for fixed-wing aircraft. The latter would be less vulnerable than helicopters to ground fire, especially from such hand-held rockets as the Soviets' formidable SA-7 Strela missile. However, the Strela does pose a threat to any low flying aircraft, as does the SA-6 Gainful, which was used so spectacularly in the Arab-Israeli war of 1973. Fixed-wing planes also have great range, firepower, and payload capacity and are more suitable than helicopters as vehicles for the delivery of "smart" bombs.

Awareness of the need for greater close air support is already apparent in the substantial pressure within the Air Force for procurement of the A-10. The USAF is at present planning to buy 730 of these relatively inexpensive close support aircraft, of which 360 would be "on line" in five tactical air wings. The A-10 would be a major step toward fulfilling close air support requirements in Europe, although whether or not they would replace existing aircraft is a question that is as yet unresolved.

Some Air Force spokesmen have opposed any decrease in supremacy/interdiction capabilities and therefore strongly favor adding A-10 wings to the present twenty-one combat tactical air wings. Prospects for the emergence of a new tactical air doctrine geared to the realities of a short war in Europe are slim under the add-on approach since more often than not changes in thinking have followed rather than preceded changes in hardware. Moreover, a proposal to increase the number of wings would undoubtedly face powerful opposition in Congress.

Some observers believe that only by replacing existing wings with A-10 wings is there reasonable hope for doctrinal revision. A tactical air force of twenty-one wings, of which say eight[1] or more were oriented exclusively toward close support, would provide a strong impetus for a new tactical air strategy.

Under a close support posture, counter air missions would not be totally neglected but would be aimed at winning *local* air superiority over the battle area. Close support missions require protection from marauding enemy fighters, and this cover could be provided either by the remaining wings of F-4s or more efficiently by wings of the proposed new Lightweight Fighter (LWF).[2] It should be noted that both the LWF and the A-10 would be far less costly than the multipurpose aircraft presently in use and thus together would probably be as effective as the current tactical air force but at less expense.

Measures to reduce the on-base vulnerability of U.S. aircraft deployed in Europe would also help to meet the requirements of a short war. On the assumption that the Pact would strike first, the likelihood that U.S. and Western European tactical air forces would be outnumbered in combat places a premium on protecting Western aircraft on the ground. Though some progress has been made to this end, present revetment construction programs should be expanded to cover all first-line aircraft deployed on the continent. As a further measure, planes should be dispersed on a larger number of airfields than is now the case. The

1. Five wings of A-10s plus the present three wings of A-7s, the only aircraft now in the active inventory highly suited for close support.

2. This is not to imply that the close air support aircraft would be totally insulated from enemy fighters; that would be impossible. In the short war scenario envisioned, losses to ground and air forces on both sides would almost certainly be great, and the United States should be prepared to absorb high attrition rates under any strategy.

concentration of the bulk of U.S. and allied tactical air power on less than one hundred Western European airfields is a highly destabilizing element in the continental military balance since it invites preemptive attack. More airfields could be provided by adapting some existing commercial fields to military use and by building smaller austere airstrips for temporary use similar to those that have served Pact tactical air forces so well.

The great mobility of modern aircraft suggests another possible hedge against a preemptive strike: the return of some tactical air squadrons to the United States. Candidates for transfer would certainly include squadrons whose capacity to carry out their assigned missions would not be materially affected by their return to the United States.[3] For example, perhaps two of the three Europe-based squadrons of F-111s, whose main tasks are long-range interdiction and delivery of tactical nuclear weapons, could be returned since, if anything, their presence on the continent (in England) increases their vulnerability to destruction. Some reconnaissance squadrons might also be removed. Squadrons redeployed to the United States would, of course, escape any surprise attack in Europe; on the other hand, if NATO's presumption as to warning time is valid, they could be returned to the continent before the outbreak of hostilities.

3. The A-10s and LWFs would not be returned. Indeed, if U.S. tactical air forces are to undergo the proposed substantial restructuring (that is, if large numbers of short-range, specialized aircraft are adopted), the need for forward basing may be increased, not reduced.

CHAPTER EIGHT

PERSPECTIVES ON THE ALTERNATIVE U.S. FORCE POSTURE

U.S. military personnel levels in the European geographical area have fluctuated substantially during the past twenty-five years in response to crises, both on the continent and elsewhere, as well as to a relaxation of political tensions. The varying figures in Table 8-1 strongly suggest the impossibility of arriving at a "magic" number of troops that could be said to represent precisely the requirements of a particular military strategy in Europe. It is curious, for example, that U.S. conventional force levels in Europe during the era of massive retaliation were generally higher than those that have been maintained since a policy of flexible response was adopted.

The authors nevertheless believe that emphasis on short war and on the improvement in the short-war fighting and deterrent capabilities of U.S. forces in NATO Center stemming from the changes proposed in this study is not incompatible with further reductions in manpower beyond those proposed in earlier chapters. These reductions might be termed "efficiency cuts" for they could legitimately be undertaken in response to congressional pressures for troop reductions but would not be of such a magnitude as to jeopardize the defense of the Central Region or to erode the bargaining position of the United States at the mutual and balanced force reductions (MBFR) conference.

Reducing U.S. Forces in NATO Center

The authors believe that the following suggested reductions are the most that U.S. forces in the Central Region could sustain while, at the same time, maintaining the "muscle" needed to meet the requirements of the present strategy of flexible response. Only reductions in ground and tactical air forces are considered.

Table 8-1. U.S. Military Personnel in the European Geographical Area, 1950–74[a]

Year	Personnel (thousands)	Year	Personnel (thousands)
1950	145	1963	380
1951	346	1964	374
1952	405	1965	363
1953	427	1966	366
1954	404	1967	337
1955	405	1968	316
1956	398	1969	300
1957	393	1970[b]	296
1958	380	1971[c]	314
1959	380	1972[c]	300
1960	379	1973[d]	313
1961	417	1974[e]	319
1962	416		

Sources: *Hearings before the Special Subcommittee on North Atlantic Treaty Organization Commitments of the House Committee on Armed Services*, 92 Cong. 1 and 2 sess. (1972), p. 12513; and *Fiscal Year 1974 Authorization for Military Procurement, Research and Development, Construction Authorization for the Safeguard ABM, and Active Duty and Selected Reserve Strengths*, Hearings before the Senate Committee on Armed Services, 93 Cong. 1 sess. (1973), Pt. 8, pp. 5282, 5284.

a. Data are for the end of the calendar year, except where otherwise noted, and are rounded, They include personnel both land-based and afloat.

b. September.

c. June.

d. March.

e. Estimated.

The Berlin Brigade

The U.S. Army, Europe (USAREUR) contains Division Forces, Special Mission Forces, and General Support Forces. Earlier analysis has established that a restructuring of USAREUR Division Forces in NATO Center would permit them to be reduced by 11,000 men. That leaves the major Special Mission Forces in Europe, which are the 3,900-man Berlin Brigade and the 22,900-man Missile Forces.

The value of the Berlin Brigade is political rather than military since its location would preclude it from playing any role in the defense of NATO Center in the event of hostilities. However, its peacetime importance as a tangible symbol of U.S. commitment to the city's protection, as well as to the Four Power Agreement on Berlin, argues against its complete removal. It is significant, however, that the United Kingdom and France maintain much smaller forces in Berlin. The authors therefore suggest a one-third reduction in the size of the Berlin Brigade. This modest cut would lower U.S. military visibility at a time of East-West progress on the Berlin question and still leave a force there adequate for meeting the U.S. commitment.

USAREUR Missile Forces

USAREUR Missile Forces have all the land-based tactical nuclear missiles deployed in West Germany. The positioning of these and other tactical nuclear weapons in Europe by the United States was originally justified as a means of offsetting what was perceived as an overwhelming communist preponderance in conventional forces. Later, under the doctrine of flexible response, tactical nuclear weapons were judged to be the crucial link between conventional defense, should it fail, and the U.S. willingness to employ its strategic deterrent, thus enhancing the credibility of that deterrent.[1]

These basic rationales still prevail although recent developments have raised serious doubts about their validity. First, the increasing realization that the conventional military balance in Europe is not hopelessly unfavorable to NATO and that it does not preclude a successful nonnuclear defense of Western Europe has served to diminish the relative importance of tactical nuclear weapons in NATO strategy. Once perceived as sufficient only to provide a "pause" before a nuclear response, NATO's conventional forces are now considered by many to be capable of halting and containing a Pact invasion without resort to nuclear weapons.

Moreover, the growing recognition of the inevitably disastrous effects of a tactical nuclear exchange in Central Europe has discernibly reduced the willingness of NATO to provoke one. This doubt is well founded since it is highly unlikely that a mutual use of nuclear weapons could be confined to selected military targets with relatively little collateral damage, both because military and civilian targets are difficult to separate in the heavily populated Central Region and because the Soviet Union continues to rely on tactical nuclear weapons that are much more indiscriminate and "dirty" than those of the United States. Unless the USSR failed to respond in kind, a first use of tactical nuclear weapons by

1. For two brief but informative discussions of the evolution of tactical nuclear doctrine with respect to Europe, see Morton H. Halperin, *Defense Strategies for the Seventies* (Little, Brown, 1971), pp. 103–12; and Jeffrey Record, "U.S. Tactical Nuclear Weapons in Europe: 7,000 Warheads in Search of a Rationale," *Arms Control Today*, Vol. 4 (April 1974).

NATO could lead to the destruction of the European society that the Atlantic Alliance is designed to protect.

The problem is compounded by a lack of conclusive evidence that the Soviets discriminate between a tactical and a strategic nuclear war—at least with respect to a major conflagration in Europe. Recognition of the potential gradations of conflict above the nuclear threshold that characterizes flexible response is not apparent in Russian military doctrine. The destructiveness of their own tactical nuclear weapons clearly impedes the ability to make such finite distinctions. Indeed, an admission that a war in Europe need not inevitably be a nuclear one—involving a strategic exchange between the United States and the USSR—is relatively new in Soviet military thinking. Even though the Soviets accept the possibility of a conventional-war phase in a major conflict on the continent, they continue to make little distinction publicly among the various levels of nuclear war that might follow. This may well reflect the not unreasonable conviction that once *any* nuclear weapon is detonated in Europe, both the confusion and the hysteria that would probably follow and the fear of being preempted at successive levels of conflict would generate irresistible pressures for rapid escalation.

In addition, the traditional view of tactical nuclear weapons as a suitable substitute for manpower has been challenged by a number of analysts who argue convincingly that a tactical nuclear environment would require larger forces because the battle area would be vastly expanded and because losses would be much higher than in a conventional conflict.[2] Even in peacetime, the maintenance and protection of deployed tactical nuclear weapons require sizable manpower resources that could

2. General Matthew B. Ridgway reached these conclusions as early as 1956 (*Soldier: The Memoirs of Matthew B. Ridgway* [Harper, 1956], pp. 296–97):

"There are a number of sound and logical reasons why a field army of the atomic age may have to be bigger than its predecessors. . . . The complex new weapons themselves—the atomic cannon, rockets, and guided missiles—require far more men to serve and maintain them than did the simpler field pieces of World War II and Korea. The prospect of sudden and enormous casualties, inflicted by the enemy with his own new weapons, makes necessary the training of replacements in great numbers for the dead, and a medical establishment larger than ever to care for the sick and wounded. In the main, though, the changing shape of the battlefield itself sets the requirements for more men. The battle zones of World War II within which actual ground combat took place were rarely as much as twenty-five miles in depth. Penetrations of armored and airborne forces in the battle areas of the future may well extend two hundred miles or even more depth, and only by great dispersion, in the wars of the future, will ground elements be able to survive."

otherwise be devoted to strengthening the conventional deterrent. This is certainly the case with U.S. forces in Europe; at present, for example, about 10 percent of USAREUR's total manpower is assigned to the Missile Forces.

Finally, Russia's achievement of rough strategic parity with the United States at least raises a question as to the value of tactical nuclear deployments as a link to the strategic deterrent. Recognition of this fact, of course, lay behind Gaullist assertions in the mid-1960s that NATO Europe could not depend on the U.S. nuclear guarantee. And it continues to generate suspicions in Europe about the "nuclear" reliability of the United States.

This suggests that the official rationales underlying present tactical nuclear deployments in the European theater are less persuasive than they once were. If, as the authors have argued, Europe *is* defensible by conventional means—and can be made more so by changing the structure and disposition of U.S. forces that are available for combat on the continent—then it would appear that tactical nuclear weapons serve only as a hedge against *unexpected* failure. Yet resort to a widespread tactical nuclear response under any circumstances, even if it did not provoke direct Soviet retaliation against the United States, would gravely endanger the very Europe that NATO seeks to defend.

What, therefore, might be the role of tactical nuclear weapons under the proposed new U.S. force posture? If, as is claimed, the usefulness of the weapons in NATO Center is diminishing, then the authors believe that a cut of at least 25 percent in Missile Forces may be made. This would leave behind a stockpile large enough to maintain the nuclear option across the spectrum of possible conflicts so as to cause the Warsaw Pact to make adjustments for tactical uncertainty. In addition, removing air-delivered tactical nuclear weapons to the United States—unless they were eliminated from the arsenal—would not preclude a tactical nuclear response in Europe since airlift would permit their rapid redeployment to the continent. Even under current strategy the number of forward-deployed warheads can and should be reduced. The 7,000 located in Europe at present not only are more than needed for an effective response, but also severely complicate the command, control, and security problems associated with Europe-deployed systems.

There are powerful political reasons for not taking action that would be construed by U.S. allies as "denuclearizing" Europe. They perceive tactical nuclear weapons as a powerful element of deterrence. This perception need not, however, preclude modest cuts on grounds of efficiency.

Other Special Mission Forces and General Support Forces

Other Special Mission Forces and General Support Forces in Europe contain strategic intelligence and security units and units performing logistic and base support as well as other joint and combined functions. These forces, which contain approximately 17,000 men, might be reduced by 20 percent if more use were made of multinational operations —not only in the logistics field, as suggested, but also in base operations, communications, intelligence, and security.

Implications of Additional Force Cuts

Table 8-2 shows the current U.S. Army strength in Europe and the proposed reductions. Of the suggested total cut of 21,600 (about 11 percent of all U.S. Army forces now in Europe), the Division Force reduction of 11,000 has been analyzed above for savings. Based on earlier calculations, a withdrawal of 10,600 more Army troops, plus a proportionate share of dependents (about 5,300), from Europe to the United States would save an estimated additional $2.7 million in annual operating costs peculiar to Europe and another $74 million in balance-of-payments costs. Since some Special Mission Forces are structured for specific missions, reducing the scope of those missions should permit the complete elimination of the manpower spaces from the Army. Hence, an additional 7,200 Army spaces might be eliminated as a result of the Berlin Brigade and Missile Force reductions. Using the 93 percent manning estimate and the 0.35 space reduction in the General Support and Trained Individuals categories for each individual cut from the Special

Table 8-2. Proposed Reductions in U.S. Army Forces in Europe

Force	*Current manpower*	*Proposed manpower*	*Change*
Division Forces[a]	155,000	144,000	−11,000
Berlin Brigade	3,900	2,600	− 1,300
Missile Forces	22,900	17,000	− 5,900
Other special missions and general support forces	17,000	13,600	− 3,400
Total	198,800	177,200	−21,600

a. Divisions, initial supporting increments, and sustaining supporting increments.

Mission Forces, Army manpower levels might be reduced by a total of 9,000 more individuals, with an annual saving in Army operating costs of approximately $134 million.

Possible reductions in U.S. Air Forces in Europe (USAFE), which currently contain approximately 50,000 military and civilian personnel, should also be studied. The authors believe that a two-step reduction of about 13 percent warrants further study, especially since Air Force requirements have not been analyzed here. Among the actions that might be considered in the initial step are several that would reduce manpower by about 4,000 spaces without jeopardizing a responsive combat capability in the event of an emergency. These might include:

- Combining appropriate command and control functions of the 2nd and 4th Allied Tactical Air Forces. (This could save manpower in allied air forces as well.)
- Reducing headquarters staff overhead in USAFE and the subordinate 3rd, 16th, and 17th Air Forces.
- Consolidating air rescue and recovery forces as a joint NATO function.
- Consolidating, in a joint command, tactical airlift support provided to NATO allies.
- Using more joint basing arrangements, which would result in air base support by NATO allies, particularly in the Federal Republic of Germany.
- Removing one tactical reconnaissance squadron from NATO Center to the United States with plans for its return to Europe in an emergency, under the "bare base" concept.
- Consolidating to a greater extent aircraft control and warning activities under joint NATO control.

A second step would reduce USAFE manpower by approximately 2,700 additional spaces. This step would cut into combat air power; however, in view of present strategy for NATO Center, the expectation of political warning time, and the mobility of air force units using "bare base" concepts, the risk involved in the additional cuts is considered small. The reductions could be achieved by removing two F-111 tactical fighter squadrons and two more tactical reconnaissance squadrons (RF-4Cs) from deployed status in Europe. Their forward bases could be placed on standby status, and the squadrons would be postured for immediate deployment from the United States if it were necessary. The "bare base" concept for support of squadrons could be used in lieu of standby bases.

Removing two F-111 squadrons would still leave one squadron deployed at Upper Heyford, England. As for tactical reconnaissance, removing two more squadrons of RF-4Cs would still leave three squadrons of tactical reconnaissance aircraft forward-deployed, a force that the authors feel would be adequate for initial use in a crisis until additional squadrons could return to bases in Europe.

The saving in annual operating costs that would result from a reduction in Air Force manpower in Europe and redeployment to the United States would be minimal, as in the case of Army manpower. However, if the USAFE spaces were eliminated entirely from the force, substantial savings would accrue. For example, if the Air Force eliminated say 3,000 of the 4,000 spaces removed from Europe in step one, an annual cost saving of about $77.5 million in fiscal 1974 dollars would be achieved.[3]

Budgetary Consequences

This study has sought to investigate ways in which U.S. ground and tactical air forces available at present for NATO contingencies could be geared more effectively to what the authors believe is the most likely threat in Europe—namely, a short war of great intensity. The primary focus has been on ground forces deployable in the Central Region. It should be emphasized that the proposed changes in the U.S. force posture are based on existing strategy and present active force levels. The question whether the defense of Western Europe could be achieved with different strategies, calling for reduced or larger U.S. force levels than are now maintained, is not considered.

With these limitations in mind, the authors believe that their proposed alternative U.S. force posture in NATO promises a military establishment that would be better attuned to the more likely threat in Europe and that would mean substantial long-term budgetary and balance-of-payments savings. Redisposing U.S. forces on the continent, increasing the readiness of reinforcements via categorization of divisions, dispersing prepositioned equipment, reorganizing combat service support—all would serve to create a U.S. military response much more

3. Based on a fiscal 1974 budget estimate of $4.6 billion for Air Force General Purpose Forces in Program 2 (including procurement, military construction, pay, and operations and maintenance costs in Program 2) and an Air Force fiscal 1974 manpower estimate for Program 2 of 177,000.

Table 8-3. Summary of Proposed Force Changes and Cost Implications
Millions of fiscal 1974 dollars

Modification	*Saving in annual operating cost*	*Initial investment cost (maximum)*	*Balance-of-payments saving*
Restructure active and reserve component forces by division category			
Change force composition	...	+725.0	...
Reduce active manpower by 14,900 spaces	−221.5	...	...
Reduce reserve manpower by 35,000 spaces	−125.0	...	...
Transfer 9,000 active Marines to Reserve	− 72.0	...	...
Reduce Division Forces in Europe by 11,000 spaces (plus 5,500 dependents)	− 3.0[a]	...	− 77.0
Military construction for 5,500 dependents	...	+ 37.0	...
Estimated reduction of 119,000 reserve component spaces resulting from multinational logistics command participation	−426.0	...	...
Rotate Army units in Europe			
Remove 9,500 more dependents	...	...	− 44.0
Military construction for 9,500 dependents	...	+ 63.0	...
Airlift cost of unit rotation	+ 47.2	...	...
Joint basing[b]	−150.0	...	...
Reduce special mission and general support forces in Europe			
Remove 10,600 more troops and 5,300 more dependents	− 2.7[a]	...	− 74.0
Military construction for 5,300 dependents	...	+ 35.0	...
Reduce active manpower by 9,000 spaces	−134.0	...	...
Credit for housing not needed for 7,200 special mission spaces that have been eliminated	...	− 24.0	...
Reduce Air Force structure by 3,000 spaces	− 77.0	...	− 20.0
Total	−1,164.0[c]	+836.0[d]	−215.0[c]

a. Costs peculiar to Europe.
b. Assumes one-third of U.S. Army, Europe, is on joint bases and that host pays 75 percent of base operating support costs.
c. Annual.
d. One time.

sensitive to the requirements of a short, intense war than is now the case. Moreover, the authors' suggested modifications of U.S. forces both in Europe and in the United States would result in overall annual budgetary savings of approximately $1.2 billion in fiscal year 1974 dollars. Table 8-3 summarizes the force modifications and cost implications. Proposed cuts in forces deployed in Europe would also reduce dollar outflows associated with U.S. troops on the continent by at least $215 million a year. Additional balance-of-payments savings, stemming from reductions achieved through extensive joint basing and the creation of a multinational logistics command, could run as high as $300 million.

In the short term, of course, budgetary economies would be offset at least partially by the one-time equipment procurement and new military construction costs of restructuring U.S. ground forces, estimated at about $836 million. Structuring for a short war in NATO Center would also entail certain one-time investments in new equipment by the Air Force, although here too there would be subsequent annual savings since the long-term costs of procuring and operating such weapons systems at the A-10 and the Lightweight Fighter should be less than those of maintaining the more expensive aircraft that now dominate the U.S. tactical air inventory. And in fact new weapons systems for the Air Force will not be effective just for NATO contingencies; they will increase military capability for meeting other conventional threats and contingencies. However, estimates of the costs that would be involved in a major restructuring of U.S. tactical air forces and the procurement of new systems are beyond the scope of this study.

The prospect of achieving a more tactically realistic and efficient U.S. military presence in Europe, with fewer troops and at less expense, should be an attractive one to Congress, which is concerned with what is increasingly perceived as an unwieldy and excessive allocation of U.S. military resources to the defense of Europe. Moreover, if adopted, the new force posture would serve to strengthen NATO's position at the MBFR talks, since the more formidable military strength inherent in the new force posture would be clearly discerned by the Soviet Union.

Managing Change within the Alliance

Less clear is how America's NATO allies would feel about the new posture. Although it has long been recognized on the continent that a short war is more likely than a long one, the response of Western European governments to many of the proposed changes in the U.S. force posture would probably be unenthusiastic. Many of those governments tend to equate any reduction of U.S. troops on the continent with a weakening of U.S. resolve to defend Europe, despite the fact that past fluctuations in troop levels have had no such effect. Others might feel that *increased* emphasis on U.S. conventional capabilities in Europe would reduce the credibility of the strategic deterrent. Certain to encounter resistance from many governments and national military establishments would be the proposals for joint basing arrangements, redisposing U.S. forces, and a multinational logistics command, all of which would require a greater degree of interdependence than now exists. Past successful opposition to similar proposals suggests the difficulty of making military changes in the face of a threat that seems remote and of launching new joint ventures in an environment of widening national differences. On the other hand, the proposals to increase the number of U.S. divisions in Europe from four to six and to place a greater emphasis on close air support would be well received on the continent.

European reactions would depend in part on how these proposals were put forward. They would stand the greatest chance of acceptance if they resulted from inter-allied consultation on how to meet NATO's changing needs, instead of being advanced as full-blown proposals, much less announced as decisions, by the United States. During this inter-allied consultation, the United States would have an opportunity to convince its European allies that the proposed changes in U.S. force posture were designed to improve this country's ability to meet the most likely threat. The authors believe that a thoughtful evaluation of all of the elements of the suggested new posture would lead to this conclusion. For many reasons, however, this view might not emerge from inter-allied consultation. If NATO agreement on these changes could not be secured, it would be counterproductive for the United States to try to put them into effect. For one thing, their execution depends in some cases on allied cooperation. For another, to make them in the face of allied opposition would threaten the unity on which Western European security is so vitally dependent.

The proposals put forward here make sense in terms of military effectiveness and of saving men and money, and are responsive to congressional concerns. Whether they also make sense in terms of allied attitudes and are responsive to allied desires can be ascertained only through a long process of consultation. The authors of this study believe that this process should now be undertaken.

Non-U.S. NATO Ground Forces Available for Combat in the Central Region

Table A-1 shows the postulated buildup of division equivalents in the Central Region by non-U.S. NATO countries during the 120-day period following a decision to mobilize. For these countries, two cases are considered; the primary difference between them is that the second includes forces not formally committed to NATO. In Case I—the less favorable one—only those national forces (expressed in division equivalents) that are committed to NATO are included. All available division equivalents of Belgium, West Germany, the Netherlands, and a part of the French First Army located in West Germany are included because of their proximity to the zone of action, as are the NATO-committed forces of the United Kingdom and Canada. In the more favorable Case II, however, an attempt is made to postulate what forces from the various national commands—in addition to those listed in Case I—are expected to be available to reinforce the buildup. The assessment below for each NATO ally deployed in the Central Region details the sources of both Case I and Case II force levels.

Belgium

The Belgian Army has an active strength of 71,500. Case I contributions to NATO consist of one corps of two division equivalents: one armored brigade, three motorized infantry brigades, two reconnaissance battalions, and a paracommando regiment. Additional forces available under Case II are rapidly mobilizable ready reserves of 120,000 men, formed into one mechanized brigade, one motorized infantry brigade, independent territorial defense units, and additional logistics support units. It is estimated that these reserves should contribute approximately

Table A-1. Mobilization of European and Canadian NATO Ground Forces for Combat in the Central Region, M Day through M + 120, Favorable and Unfavorable Cases

Division equivalents

	M day[a]		*M + 7*		*M + 15*		*M + 30*		*M + 60*		*M + 90*		*M + 120*	
Country	*I*[b]	*II*[c]	*I*[b]	*II*[c]	*I*[b]	*II*[c]	*I*[b]	*II*[c]	*I*[b]	*II*[c]	*I*[b]	*II*[c]	*I*[b]	*II*[c]
Belgium	2	2	2	2	2	2	3	3	3	3	3	3	3	3
Canada	$\frac{1}{3}$	$\frac{1}{3}$	$\frac{1}{3}$	$\frac{1}{3}$	$\frac{1}{3}$	$\frac{1}{3}$	$\frac{1}{3}$	1	$\frac{1}{3}$	1	$\frac{1}{3}$	1	$\frac{1}{3}$	1
France	2	2	5	5	5	5	5	7	5	10	5	10	5	10
Federal Republic of Germany	11	11	14	14	14	14	14	14	14	14	14	14	14	14
Netherlands	2	2	2	2	2	2	3	3	3	3	3	3	3	3
United Kingdom	3	3	3	3	3	3	3	4	3	5	3	5	3	5
Total	20$\frac{1}{3}$	20$\frac{1}{3}$	26$\frac{1}{3}$	26$\frac{1}{3}$	26$\frac{1}{3}$	26$\frac{1}{3}$	28$\frac{1}{3}$	32	28$\frac{1}{3}$	36	28$\frac{1}{3}$	36	28$\frac{1}{3}$	36

Sources: International Institute for Strategic Studies, *The Military Balance 1972–1973* (London: IISS, 1972); T. N. Dupuy and Wendell Blanchard, *The Almanac of World Military Power*, 2d ed. (T. N. Dupuy Associates, 1972); *The Force Structure in the Federal Republic of Germany: Analysis and Options: Summary* (Bonn: Report of the Force Structure Commission to the Government of the Federal Republic of Germany, 1972); *White Paper 1971/1972: The Security of the Federal Republic of Germany and the Development of the Federal Armed Forces*, published in Bonn by the Federal Minister of Defense on Behalf of the German Federal Government (1971); *French White Paper on National Defense, Volume I* (New York, Ambassade de France, Service de Presse et d'Information, 1972); and Donald S. MacDonald, Minister of National Defence, *Defence in the 70's: White Paper on Defence* (Ottawa: Information Canada, 1971).

a. The day on which mobilization begins. European and Canadian NATO divisions located in the Central Region, including the two French divisions in the Federal Republic of Germany, are presumed to be available on M day. For this analysis the length of time between M day and D day is not specified.

b. In Case I the circumstances are less favorable to NATO because only forces that are formally committed to NATO at present are included. Some French forces are also excluded.

c. In Case II the circumstances are more favorable to NATO because all forces potentially available to NATO are counted, including those not formally committed to the alliance.

one additional division equivalent ready for commitment to NATO Center within thirty days of mobilization. There are 500,000 additional trained reservists available for mobilization as replacements.

Canada

The active portion of the Canadian Army has a strength of 33,000 men. NATO-committed forces consist of one mechanized combat group containing three mechanized infantry battalions, one reconnaissance regiment, and one light artillery battalion—the equivalent of about one-third of a division. In Canada one airmobile combat group forms a reinforcing element for the Allied Command Europe Mobile Force, which can be used on the northern flank as required by the Supreme Allied Commander, Europe (SACEUR). Other major national command forces in Canada consist of two mechanized combat groups, organized similarly to the NATO-committed group, and one airborne regiment. It is likely that in a European crisis Canada would release the two mechanized combat groups for deployment to NATO Center as reinforcements. Hence, in Case II, one Canadian division equivalent has been postulated as available by M + 30. There are about 19,000 Canadian Army reserves, and they are organized for mobilization on short notice. It is not assumed that they will provide additional units for the Canadian commitment within the first 120 days, but they are considered as replacements to be used when needed.

France

The French First Army has two mechanized divisions in West Germany, which probably could not escape combat involvement at the outset of a conflict there. They are therefore considered to be available on M day. The rest of the French First Army is located in France and is charged with the defense of the frontier or intervention outside French territory, as directed. The units in France consist of three mechanized divisions and two corps headquarters and corps support units. The proximity and mission of these units suggest that within M + 7 the entire French First Army (five divisions) would be committed to NATO Center. As a strategic reserve, the French Army maintains a parachute division and one air-portable motorized brigade.

The Territorial Defense Force (DOT), another major element of the French ground forces, contains two alpine brigades, two motorized infantry regiments, four armored car regiments, one parachute battalion, and twenty-five infantry battalions. The Army supplies most of the DOT's forces although the Gendarmerie makes a large contribution. The location of DOT forces and their geographical organization by military districts makes them ideally suited for providing close liaison with reserve forces; indeed, a "plan is being developed to link mobilized [reserve] units to the standing forces of the DOT."[1] The DOT consists of a skeleton division structure in each of France's eight military districts, with one or two regular battalions plus other units that would be expanded in an emergency by reservists within each district. Upon mobilization, those units would be prepared to defend national territory and the highly sensitive areas in which the elements of France's Strategic Nuclear Force are located. DOT forces also would be available to participate, as needed, with the French First Army in the intervention

1. *French White Paper on National Defense: Volume I,* p. 19.

role in Europe.[2] Thus some DOT forces may be considered available for the defense of NATO Center.

There are 450,000 French Army reserves, who are trained and available for immediate mobilization. They are organized into eighty infantry battalions and five armored car regiments, designed to fill out divisional structures in their respective military districts. An assessment of strategic reserve and DOT units available for deployment to NATO Center to reinforce the French First Army strongly suggests that in Case II, two additional divisions could be committed by M + 30 and at least three more by M + 60. This expectation is supported in an article by Delbert Fowler, who credits France with five reinforcing divisions for NATO in addition to the five that would be available from the French First Army.[3]

Federal Republic of Germany[4]

The West German Army is a combination of two forces that were merged in 1969: the Field Army (248,000 effectives), consisting of three corps made up of a total of twelve divisions, plus nonorganic support; and the Territorial Army (consisting of a proposed 66,000 men), whose major units, when the reorganization now in progress is completed, will contain six Home Defense Groups, combat support and service units, and security companies for local defense.[5] Each Home Defense Group will be mobile and of brigade size (about 7,000 men)

2. Ibid., p. 24.

3. Delbert M. Fowler, "How Many Divisions? A NATO-Warsaw Pact Assessment," *Military Review,* Vol. 52 (November 1972), pp. 76–88.

4. Information on FRG Army organization and missions is contained in *White Paper 1971/1972: The Security of the Federal Republic of Germany and the Development of the Federal Armed Forces,* published in Bonn by the Federal Minister of Defense on Behalf of the German Federal Government (1971); and *The Force Structure in the Federal Republic of Germany: Analysis and Options: Summary* (Report of the Force Structure Commission to the Government of the Federal Republic of Germany, 1972).

5. A recent, conflicting assessment appeared in the *International Defense Review* ("Bonn Report," Vol. 7 [February 1974]), which declared that the peacetime strength of the German Army (field and territorial components) is calculated to be 495,000. The present strength of the Bundeswehr after mobilization of reserves was estimated at 1.2 million men. No definitive explanation for the active force discrepancy is available except possibly differing perceptions by the analysts of the degree of active status of some of the forces.

and will have substantial anti-tank capabilities. The merger is nearing completion and was undertaken to promote the forward defense of West Germany's borders.

The NATO-committed Field Army will have the primary missions of defending the country's border and providing mobile reserve forces to contain and repel major enemy penetrations. With respect to training, control, and logistics functions, the Territorial Army will be closely tied to the Field Army and will have the missions of: (1) securing rear areas and lines of communication, (2) defending key areas and installations locally, (3) providing blocking forces against enemy penetrations, and (4) assuring freedom of maneuver for all NATO forces operating on West German territory. The Territorial Army will remain under national command in an emergency; however, its integration with NATO-committed forces of the Federal Republic of Germany (FRG) will assure closely coordinated operations.

The Mommer Commission on Force Structure in the FRG, which completed its study in 1972, has recommended a Field Army of twenty-four full-strength brigades (M-day capability) and twelve cadre-strength brigades for training (M + 3 capability, with augmentation from the reserves) to round out its twelve-division force. If the Commission's proposals are adopted, the Territorial Army, in addition to its six Home Defense Groups, will contain three hundred motorized security companies for local defense, with a readiness capability of M + 3. The Commission's recommendations have official government support and are now before the Bundestag.[6] The proposed new force structure, if approved, could be realized by 1975. Augmented by federal contingent authority to requisition civilian vehicles and other needed equipment, the structure is expected to foster a more responsive and better trained fighting force than West Germany now fields. For example, brigades of the German Army currently consist of about 65 percent of fully trained active troops, 15 percent of draftees undergoing their first three months of training, and 20 percent of trained reservists on three-day call-up.

West German Army reserves number approximately 1.8 million, of which about 540,000 under the proposed new force structure would be

6. It is known that planners in the FRG Defense Ministry currently favor thirty-six brigades of close to full strength. Some battalions in the active brigades would be at reduced strength, but with on-call reserve augmentation that would allow readiness objectives to meet NATO requirements. Accordingly, the duration of on-call reserve status would be extended from three months to one year.

available for immediate mobilization to fill out the reduced strength units of the regular Army and to bring units of the Territorial Army to full strength by M + 3. About eleven division equivalents are expected to be immediately available in NATO Center, and by M + 3 an enhanced reserve readiness should guarantee the equivalent of no less than three additional divisions.

The Netherlands

The Dutch have an active army of about 76,000 men. NATO-committed forces consist of one corps of two armored and four mechanized brigades. A small number of active army units also have been designated for territorial defense under national command. Trained reserves number 350,000, of which 40,000 are immediately mobilizable into one infantry division plus supporting units. Additional brigades for territorial defense could be mobilized from other trained reservists. Former Netherlands Defense Minister de Koster recently revealed a plan for reorganizing the Royal Netherlands Army (RNA) that would retain the six combat-ready and four mobilizable brigades in the current structure but would mechanize all but three of the RNA's infantry battalions and would identically structure armored and mechanized infantry brigades. Measures to increase the readiness of reserve forces also have been announced. The addition of reserves that are more rapidly mobilizable should increase the RNA's commitment to NATO from two divisions to three by M + 30. Indeed, if the reorganization plan is implemented, a three-division force might be ready by M + 15.

United Kingdom

The active army of Great Britain contains about 176,500 effectives. NATO-committed forces consist of about 55,000 men in one corps, which is made up of three divisions, plus corps support. Located in Great Britain are two major commands containing additional national forces: a Strategic Reserve of three air-portable infantry brigades, two parachute battalions, and one commando regiment; and the United Kingdom Command, consisting of about eighteen battalions. Two brigade headquarters and one armored reconnaissance regiment are also stationed in the United Kingdom but are oriented toward operations in Northern Ireland.

British reserves fall into three categories: Regular Army Reserves (120,000), with specific mobilization assignments; Army General Reserves (177,000), who have no specific mobilization assignments but are to be used as replacements; and Territorial and Army Volunteer Reserves (56,400), for home defense. It is known that some reserves are designated to form additional units for commitment to NATO.

A realistic assessment of active but uncommitted U.K. forces and available reserves should yield, under Case II, at least two divisions for NATO in addition to the three expected under Case I. Drawn from active forces of the Strategic Reserve and the U.K. Command, augmented by ready reserves, one should be available to NATO by M + 30, and the other, by M + 60.

APPENDIX B

Soviet and Eastern European Ground and Tactical Air Forces

This appendix presents a quantitative survey of Soviet and Eastern European ground and tactical combat air forces. Bulgaria's small and poorly equipped forces are not included in the Warsaw Pact order of battle since, for geographic and other reasons, their participation in a Pact buildup opposite NATO Center is not expected under any circumstances.

Table B-1 lists all Soviet Army divisions by location, type, and readiness. It is clear that the bulk of the Soviet Army (including about 90 percent of its armored divisions) is located west of the Urals, although large forces are maintained in the Far East. Each of the thirty-one divisions stationed in Eastern Europe is maintained at close to full strength and may be considered combat ready. Deployments in central and southern USSR are small and much understrength, suggesting a Soviet presumption of a low threat opposite those two regions.

Each Soviet division falls into one of three categories of readiness. The precise number of divisions in each category and their location remain classified information, although the open literature on the subject provides a solid foundation for reasonably accurate estimates. The characteristics of each category are better known. Category I divisions are full-strength or near full-strength formations and are considered combat ready on or about M day (the day mobilization begins). Category II divisions, manned at approximately 75 percent of their authorized strength and having all of their equipment, are believed to be fully mobilizable no earlier than M + 30.[1] Category III divisions are cadre units that need major additions of both men and equipment before they are combat ready. Since they have only about 25 percent of their re-

1. Irving Heymont and Melvin H. Rosen, "Five Foreign Army Reserve Systems," *Military Review*, Vol. 53 (March 1973), p. 35.

Table B-1. Soviet Army Divisions by Location, Readiness, and Type

Category of readiness and type of division	*Location and number of divisions*					
	Eastern Europe	*European USSR*	*Central USSR*	*Southern USSR*	*Far East*[a]	*Total*
Category I	31	12	0	0	22	65
Motorized rifle	15	2	0	0	16	33
Armored	16	5	0	0	4	25
Airborne	0	5	0	0	2	7
Category II	0	27	2	11	11	51
Motorized rifle	0	12	2	8	7	29
Armored	0	15	0	3	4	22
Airborne	0	0	0	0	0	0
Category III	0	21	6	10	11	48
Motorized rifle	0	19	4	10	11	44
Armored	0	2	2	0	0	4
Airborne	0	0	0	0	0	0
Total	31	60	8	21	44	164

Sources: Authors' calculations, based on data appearing in International Institute for Strategic Studies, *The Military Balance 1972–1973* (London: IISS, 1972), pp. 7–8; and T. N. Dupuy and Wendell Blanchard, *The Almanac of World Military Power*, 2d ed. (T. N. Dupuy Associates, 1972), pp. 150–51.
a. Far Eastern deployments include two divisions in Outer Mongolia.

quired manpower and about 50 percent of their equipment, most of which is in storage, Category III divisions are believed to be mobilizable no sooner than M + 120.[2] However, the active portions of these cadre divisions conceivably could be amalgamated to form a smaller number of new divisions that might be available for combat by M + 60.

Table B-2 presents three possible scenarios of a Warsaw Pact buildup of ground forces opposite NATO Center from M day through M + 120. General assumptions applicable to all three cases are that: (1) hostilities are not initiated throughout the period; (2) all Pact divisions that are at close to 100 percent strength (Category I) and are located in East Germany, Czechoslovakia, and Poland are available for deployment on M day; (3) Czechoslovakia's two cadre divisions are available by M + 30; (4) only two Polish divisions are at full strength on M day, with the rest available by M + 7; and (5) Soviet Category II divisions are deployed by M + 30.

2. Heymont and Rosen, in "Five Foreign Army Reserve Systems," suggest that Category III divisions could be mobilized in 90 days. The authors believe, however, that Category III divisions, because of their personnel and equipment composition, are not as quickly mobilizable as are U.S. reserve divisions, which they believe could be ready in 90 days. Hence, they have postulated a Category III division readiness of M + 120.

Table B-2. Soviet and Eastern European Ground Force Mobilization Capabilities Opposite NATO Center, from M Day through M + 120, Most Favorable, Most Likely, and Least Favorable Cases[a]

Number of divisions

	M day			*M + 7*			*M + 15*			*M + 30*			*M + 60*			*M + 90*			*M + 120*		
Country	*A*	*B*	*C*	*A*	*B*	*C*	*A*	*B*	*C*	*A*	*B*	*C*	*A*	*B*	*C*	*A*	*B*	*C*	*A*	*B*	*C*
USSR	27	27	27	31	31	31	39	37	37	59	55	55	71	67	55	76	67	55	83	74	72
Czechoslovakia	10	10	10	10	10	10	10	10	10	12	12	12	12	12	12	12	12	12	12	12	12
DDR (East Germany)	6	6	6	6	6	6	6	6	6	6	6	6	6	6	6	6	6	6	6	6	6
Poland	2	2	2	13	13	13	13	13	13	13	13	13	13	13	13	13	13	13	13	13	13
Hungary	0	0	0	4	0	0	4	0	0	4	0	0	4	0	0	4	0	0	4	0	0
Rumania	0	0	0	4	0	0	4	0	0	4	0	0	4	0	0	4	0	0	4	0	0
Total	45	45	45	68	60	60	76	66	66	98	86	86	110	98	86	115	98	86	122	105	103

Sources: Authors' calculations, based on data appearing in International Institute for Strategic Studies, *The Military Balance 1972–1973*, pp. 7–13; Dupuy and Blanchard, *The Almanac of World Military Power*, pp. 133–52; "Reinforcements for Europe," *Strategic Survey* (London: International Institute for Strategic Studies, 1973), pp. 19–23; and Irving Heymont and Melvin H. Rosen, "Five Foreign Army Reserve Systems," *Military Review*, Vol. 53 (March 1973).

a. Columns A contain data for the most favorable cases, columns B for the most likely, and columns C for the least favorable cases. See Chapter 2 for explanation of circumstances for each case.

Case A represents the most favorable circumstances for a Pact buildup because, in addition to the full participation of East German, Czech, and Polish forces, four of Hungary's seven divisions and four of Rumania's nine divisions are also deployed opposite NATO Center by M + 7, the rest remaining in their respective countries to garrison the Pact's southern flank. Moreover, the Soviet Union maximizes its deployments opposite the Center by (1) committing minimum forces to its own northern and southern flanks, (2) transferring one-third of its forces in the Far East to the Central Front or to a strategic reserve, and (3) generating by M + 60 an additional twelve divisions opposite the Center by combining the active personnel and equipment of two-thirds of its Category III divisions in the Western USSR.

Case B represents the most likely circumstances of a Pact buildup. Hungary and Rumania successfully resist Soviet pressures to contribute forces to the Pact buildup along the Central Front. The Soviet Union, while still amalgamating some of its Category III divisions, commits larger forces along its flanks (at the expense of the Center) and, presuming a willingness on the part of the Chinese to take military advantage of Soviet difficulties in Europe (thus threatening a "two-front" war), leaves its divisions in the Far East in place but designates some for use as a strategic reserve.

Case C represents the circumstances least favorable to a Pact buildup. Hungarian and Rumanian forces do not participate, nor do Soviet forces in the Far East. Moreover, the Soviet Union commits even greater forces than under Case B to its flank areas and amalgamates none of its Category III divisions, deciding instead to bring them in at M + 120.

Table B-3 presents a survey of Soviet and Eastern European tactical combat air power. The Soviet Union is, of course, the central repository of that power, and it alone has the latest and most sophisticated fighter-attack aircraft, such as the MIG-23 and MIG-25 interceptors. Little is known about the MIG-25 although the plane is believed to be roughly comparable to the American SR-71.

The Pact's extraordinary emphasis on air defense is reflected in the Soviet Union's allocation of more than 3,200 aircraft to the Soviet Air Defense Command (ADC), despite the fact that by the end of fiscal year 1974 the number of U.S. strategic bombers that it is estimated will be available for a retaliatory strike on the USSR (the "alert-maintained" 40 percent of 66 F-111s and 255 later-model B-52s) is about 130 planes. Although most of the aircraft assigned to the ADC could be used

Table B-3. Soviet and Eastern European Tactical Combat Aircraft

	Number of aircraft in active inventory			
Country	*Interceptor/ fighters*[a]	*Light attack bombers*[b]	*Attack fighter bombers*[c]	*Total*
USSR				
Tactical Air Force	1,000	2,000	3,000	6,000
Air Defense Command	3,200+	0	0	3,200+
Subtotal	4,200+	2,000	3,000	9,200+
Czechoslovakia	250	60	310	620
DDR (East Germany)	260	10	160	430
Poland	100	50	595	745
Hungary	60	20	100	180
Rumania	60	30	160	250
Subtotal	730	170	1,325	2,225
Total, Warsaw Pact countries[d]	4,930+	2,170	4,325	11,425+

Source: Dupuy and Blanchard, *The Almanac of World Military Power*, pp. 133–52.

a. Types of aircraft allocated to the interceptor role include MIG-15 "Fagot" and MIG-17 "Fresco" for Eastern European forces only), MIG-19 "Farmer," MIG-21 "Fishbed," MIG-23 "Foxbat," MIG-25 "Fearless" (at present code-named "Foxbat"), Yak-28P "Firebar," TU-28P "Fiddler," SU-7 "Fitter," and SU-11 "Flagon."

b. Includes the Il-28 "Beagle" and, for Soviet forces only, the Yak-28 "Brewer."

c. Includes the following aircraft in the fighter-bomber role: MIG-15 "Fagot" (for Czech, Polish, and Rumanian forces only), MIG-17 "Fresco," MIG-23 "Foxbat" (strike version), SU-7 "Fitter," and Yak-25 "Flashlight."

d. Excluding Bulgaria.

in other roles, the Soviets' long-standing obsession with air defense strongly suggests that the majority would be retained in the ADC even in the event of a major military crisis in Europe.

U.S. Ground Force Requirements in NATO Center

NATO (except for U.S.) and Warsaw Pact ground forces in the Central Region and, more particularly, division buildups from M day through M + 120 were discussed in Appendixes A and B. Three postulated buildups were examined for the Warsaw Pact (see Table B-2), and two for America's NATO allies (see Table A-1). Together they generate six possible scenarios for analysis. With the spectrum of Pact threats and of allied capabilities thus projected, U.S. force requirements for each contingency in NATO Center can be determined. Adding U.S. forces to those of U.S. allies permits an assessment of the aggregate relative strengths and capabilities of the Pact and NATO in the Center. The following analysis of U.S. requirements also presumes the same M day—that is, that there are national or international factors on both sides that trigger nearly simultaneous decisions to initiate full mobilization. Each side, within a matter of hours (or at most one or two days), learns of the other's intentions and takes action. While simultaneous mobilization cannot be judged at this time as the most likely prospect, current intelligence-gathering sources and even the readiness condition of Pact forces are such that some mobilization signal should quickly be apparent. If one presumes, as do the authors, that NATO decision makers will act quickly and decisively on the basis of accurate intelligence, mobilization activities should begin on each side almost simultaneously. A seven-day head start by the Pact is the most that seems likely, since to be in position to conduct an offensive that is overwhelming enough to promise quick success, the Pact would have to "tip its hand" early by visibly preparing and moving forward substantial military forces. These signals would be enough to generate mobilization orders by NATO leaders. Thus the analysis below also delinates a U.S. buildup requirement when Pact M day precedes NATO M day by no more than seven days.

Table C-1. Requirements for U.S. Division Buildup in NATO Center, M Day through M + 120[a]

Number of divisions

Scenario		*M day, Condition*[b]				*M + 7, Condition*[b]				*M + 15, Condition*[b]				*M + 30, Condition*[b]				*M + 60, Condition*[b]				*M + 90, Condition*[b]				*M + 120, Condition*[b]			
Assumption about Warsaw Pact countries	*Assumption about non-U.S. NATO allies*	*1*	*2*	*3*	*4*[c]	*1*	*2*	*3*	*4*[c]	*1*	*2*	*3*	*4*[c]	*1*	*2*	*3*	*4*[c]	*1*	*2*	*3*	*4*[c]	*1*	*2*	*3*	*4*[c]	*1*	*2*	*3*	*4*[c]
Case AI																													
Most favorable	Least favorable	10	4	3	(3)	19	10	8	(5)	24	14	12	(5)	37	24	21	11	45	31	27	16	49	33	30	18	53	37	33	21
Case AII																													
Most favorable	Most favorable	10	4	3	(3)	19	10	8	(5)	24	14	12	(5)	33	20	17	7	37	23	19	8	41	25	22	10	45	29	25	13
Case BI																													
Most likely	Least favorable	10	4	3	(3)	14	6	4	(4)	18	9	7	(5)	29	18	15	6	37	24	21	11	37	24	21	11	42	28	24	14
Case BII																													
Most likely	Most favorable	10	4	3	(3)	14	6	4	(4)	18	9	7	(5)	25	14	11	(6)	29	16	13	(7)	29	16	13	(7)	34	20	16	(7)
Case CI																													
Least favorable	Least favorable	10	4	3	(3)	14	6	4	(4)	18	9	7	(5)	29	18	15	6	29	18	15	6	29	18	15	6	41	27	23	13
Case CII																													
Least favorable	Most favorable	10	4	3	(3)	14	6	4	(4)	18	9	7	(5)	25	14	11	(6)	21	10	7	(6)	21	10	7	(6)	33	19	15	(7)

a. Assumes coincidental M days for NATO and Pact countries.

b. Conditions are defined as follows:

1. Pact-NATO division ratio never exceeds 1.5:1; NATO and Pact divisions qualitatively equal.
2. Pact-NATO division ratio never exceeds 1.5:1; NATO divisions qualitatively better than Pact divisions by 1.25:1.
3. Pact-NATO division ratio never exceeds 2:1; NATO and Pact divisions qualitatively equal.
4. Pact-NATO division ratio never exceeds 2:1; NATO divisions qualitatively better than Pact divisions by 1.25:1.

Conditions may be interpolated. The same result for U.S. divisions required under each condition can be obtained by ensuring that the product of values selected for the ratio of divisions and the relative quality of divisions is 1.5 for Condition 1; 1.875 for Condition 2; 2 for Condition 3; and 2.5 for Condition 4. For example, a division ratio of 1.75:1 and relative quality of divisions at 1.15:1 are approximately equivalent to Condition 3 (2:1 division ratio and qualitative equality, 1:1).

c. Numbers in parentheses represent a U.S. share (to the nearest whole division) of NATO divisions required in the Center for Condition 1—about 17.5 percent of the total over time. This figure was chosen because it represents the current percentage of division equivalents in place contributed by the United States. It was arbitrarily applied to some scenarios under Condition 4 since otherwise the theoretical results would show little or no need for U.S. deployments—a politically unrealistic prospect because, for the sake of alliance solidarity, the United States must provide a sizable share of NATO ground forces. For Condition 4 non-U.S. NATO forces would also be proportionally adjusted according to the requirement.

Two criteria are used to determine the number of U.S. divisions that, together with allied forces, are needed to counter the Pact forces in each scenario. One is simply the numerical ratio of opposing divisions; the second is the relative quality of opposing divisions. Each criteron is considered at two levels; thus four conditions can be described.

Condition 1 in Table C-1 represents the most severe condition for NATO, since the buildup of U.S. and allied divisions does not permit the Pact, at any stage of mobilization, a better than 1.5:1 advantage in number of divisions in any of the six scenarios. Some military analysts do believe that holding the Pact to a division superiority of no better than 1.5:1 is essential for a successful forward defense of NATO Center, at least against a surprise attack.[1] Moreover, Condition 1 also ignores the qualitative superiority of NATO divisions over those of the Pact, presuming that both are equal and postulating no advantage for better equipment, training, logistics, or communications, or for the superior morale that often characterizes forces engaged in the defense of their homeland.

Condition 2 also presumes the necessity of a 1.5:1 ratio but holds that NATO divisions are qualitatively 25 percent better than Pact divisions, thus making one and one-fourth Pact divisions equal to one NATO division in terms of real combat effectiveness. Admittedly this somewhat recondite notion of the relative worth of divisions is an intuitive conclusion with respect to inherent organizational, psychological, and matériel qualities (that is, the relative qualities of equipment, training, sustaining support, morale, and so on), but it does provide comparative total values for opposing divisions. Such an approach is not particularly suited to detailed war gaming or conflict analysis because of the impossibility of accurately quantifying values that are inherently qualititative. As a tool for aggregate assessments, however, some idea of the relative worth of divisions is of considerable value, particularly if it is based on educated judgments. In an even broader esoteric sense, one's subjective judgments of the relative quality and effectiveness of tactical air support as it contributes to the overall worth of ground forces can be incorporated in the single ratio of division quality.

Condition 3 maintains a 2:1 ratio of forces between the Pact and

1. See, for example, Timothy W. Stanley, *NATO in Transition: The Future of the Atlantic Alliance* (Praeger, 1965), Chap. 5, and Basil Henry Liddell-Hart, *Deterrent or Defense: A Fresh Look at the Western Military Position* (Praeger, 1960), p. 172.

NATO and treats opposing divisions as qualitatively equal. It is based on the assumption that, without the advantage of surprise, the Pact would need to muster an even greater superiority over the allies to have a reasonable chance of carrying NATO Center. Condition 3 is consonant with NATO's expectation of "political warning" before an attack. Warning favors the defender since it allows him to prepare the battlefield.

Condition 4 also has the 2:1 ratio, but it stipulates, as does Condition 2, a qualitative edge of 25 percent for NATO divisions. Condition 4 is thus the most favorable case for NATO and could be realized either after hostilities began, if NATO were initially successful in "wearing down" Pact units, or after a protracted buildup in which NATO's alignments took maximum advantage of their qualitative superiority.

The four conditions defined above dictate a broad spectrum of U.S. division requirements, depending on the scenario. The requirements of Condition 1 are admittedly well beyond what is politically and budgetarily feasible; the requirements of Condition 4, on the other hand, can be met in some cases by fewer forces than are presently available. (For a discussion of requirements derived at the lowest level, see note c in Table C-1 above.) Moreover, if the assumption that NATO has a 25 percent qualitative edge is unwarranted, interpolations that allow for some variations are possible under each condition. Similar results can be obtained for "divisions required" by ensuring that the product of any other values chosen for ratio of divisions and relative quality of divisions are equal to the product of assumed values; for example, a ratio of numbers of divisions of 1.75:1 (Pact–NATO) and of quality of divisions of 1:1.15 (the NATO divisions being 15 percent better) are equivalent to Condition 3. (Division ratio, 2:1; and relative division quality, 1:1.)

A study of the matrix of U.S. division buildups in Table C-1 reveals information that makes it possible to analyze requirements subjectively and to derive a feasible deployment sequence for U.S. divisions within reasonable fiscal and force constraints that also conforms to the *likely* conditions and scenarios in NATO Center.

For M day, U.S. division requirements under Condition 1 are unrealistic; under Conditions 2, 3, and 4, however, they are feasible in every scenario and in fact are somewhat less than the forces currently in place. The coincidence of M day and D day would represent a surprise attack; in that case, to be reasonably sure of containing the Pact offensive NATO would not want the ratio of Pact divisions to NATO divisions to be more unfavorable than 1.5:1. Condition 1 or 2 therefore prevails. If one assumes that NATO troops are more efficient, that their morale is better, and that their equipment, logistics support, and training are superior, NATO divisions would hold a qualitative edge over those of the Pact. Moreover, for a surprise attack, the Pact, in order to escape detection, would be compelled to limit preparations, thus increasing NATO's advantage. If a 25 percent qualitative edge for NATO is accepted, a situation consonant with Condition 2 should prevail, and its requirement for U.S. divisions (four) is both feasible and realistic for M day, regardless of scenario.

For M + 7, U.S. division requirements for all scenarios under Condition 1 are far beyond what is either politically or financially feasible; for 2 and 3 they are probably realistic in all scenarios except for the heaviest Pact buildup (the Pact's "most favorable" case); and in 4 they are feasible for all scenarios. If hostilities began at M + 7, the elapsed mobilization time would be so short as to constitute a tactical surprise against NATO; thus the Pact–NATO division ratio should not be worse than 1.5:1 if NATO is to have a reasonable chance of stopping the Pact. Condition 1 or 2 therefore prevails although, as was noted above, 1 is unrealistic. The presumption of a 25 percent qualitative edge for NATO means that approximately six U.S. divisions in place at M + 7, together with those of NATO allies, would be enough to contain a Pact attack for all scenarios except AI and AII Pact deployments (see Table C-1), which are highly unlikely in view of Soviet requirements in other regions.

For M + 15 through M + 120, Condition 1 requirements for U.S. divisions are unrealistic. The same is probably true for Condition 2, except in combination with the lightest Pact buildup and the most extensive NATO buildup (Case CII). But a D day that fell on M + 15 or later should give NATO enough warning time to strengthen its defensive positions and prepare its forces more thoroughly. Time should favor the defender, and beyond M + 15 NATO could probably anticipate a successful defense of the Center if a Pact–NATO division ratio no worse than 2:1 were assumed. Thus Conditions 3 and 4 would seem more appropriate for the time from M + 15 on. Since after M + 15, NATO is expected to reinforce with lightly armored formations containing reservists and territorial forces, it is improbable that NATO could maintain an initial 25 percent qualitative edge over the Pact. Thus beyond M + 15, it is assumed that the quality of opposing forces would tend toward equivalence (1:1); and hence Condition 3 is realistic for situations from M + 15 onward. As for non-U.S. NATO and Pact deployments, BII appears to be the most realistic scenario. NATO allies would probably be prepared to release enough additional national command forces to NATO during the critical phases preceding hostilities to "cover" the Pact's probable deployments (BI and BII). Therefore, it is from a combination of Condition 3 and Case BII that a realistic requirement for U.S. division deployments on and after M + 15 emerges.

An assessment of U.S. division requirements from M day through M + 120, based on the foregoing rationale, shows the following:

	M day	*M + 7*	*M + 15*	*M + 30*	*M + 60*	*M + 90*	*M + 120*
U.S. divisions required	4	6	7	11	13	14	18

The M + 90 and M + 120 requirements for Case BII and Condition 3 are thirteen and sixteen divisions, respectively; however, an increase to fourteen divisions on M + 90 and to eighteen by M + 120 is desirable if NATO is to maintain some planning hedge against strategic uncertainty. For example, if D day were to come during the early stages of mobilization, resulting in some losses sustained by U.S. divisions in transit to Europe, a deployment plan calling for a few more divisions than would theoretically be needed later in the buildup would be a prudent course of action. A hedge against the possibility of greater-than-expected Pact deployments would also be wise.

The U.S. division requirement developed above is based on the assumption that M days for both NATO and the Pact occur simultaneously. The discussion at the beginning of this appendix qualifies the validity of this assumption and suggests that a seven-day lead time favoring the Pact could occur. To examine the effect of that situation on the requirement for U.S. divisions, an analysis was conducted using the tactical rationale and conditions described above for simultaneous M days. The only difference was that the Pact M day was advanced by seven days. The resulting U.S. division requirement (to the nearest whole division) for NATO M day through M + 120 is as follows:[2]

	M day	*M + 7*	*M + 15*	*M + 30*	*M + 60*	*M + 90*	*M + 120*
U.S. divisions required	12	7	12	13	13	14	17

2. Mobilization of U.S. allies would also follow Pact M day by seven days. Buildup scenario BII (Pact–NATO allies) is considered likely. Straight-line interpolations of Table B-2 have been used to adjust Pact division capabilities during NATO buildups, which lag by seven days. Based on the previous rationale for conditions assumed at each buildup milestone, Condition 2 is considered for NATO M day and Condition 3 for NATO M + 7 through NATO M + 120.

When one compares this U.S. division requirement with the one for simultaneous M days, some startling conclusions emerge.

First, if the Pact had a seven-day head start and conducted a surprise attack (unlikely since mobilization would not go unnoticed) the United States would need twelve divisions in place (eight more than the four otherwise required). In terms of forces to assure a postulated balance for deterrence, this increase could not realistically be met. Thus means other than ground troops to redress the balance are required. These might include more effective barrier operations, equipment of higher quality, increased air power for close support, and any other improvements that would create a qualitative superiority of 60 to 70 percent for NATO divisions over Pact divisions at the beginning of a conflict.

Under Condition 3, if the Pact's mobilization preceded NATO's by seven days and the Pact then waited from one to four weeks longer before attacking, a total of one to five additional U.S. divisions would be needed, with the critical shortfall being at NATO's M + 15. Again, since significant U.S. divisional increases in the theater during that period are not realistic, qualitative improvements would be needed if NATO divisions were to be at least 15 percent better than Pact divisions—on the assumption that the Pact would have to have a 2:1 superiority in divisions to be successful. If the Pact had a head start of seven days in mobilizing and waited at least sixty more days before attacking, U.S. division requirements under the previous situation would be enough, together with help from NATO allies, to prevent the Pact countries from succeeding.

It is thus apparent that if the Pact should have as much as a seven-day head start in mobilizing and U.S. allies do not increase their postulated capability, the ability of the United States to achieve the buildup required to maintain a balance for deterrence is doubtful, given current resource allocations. For the postulated conditions, qualitative improvements in U.S. and allied divisions would be needed to offset the quantitative imbalance. The description that follows will thus focus on a realistic U.S. requirement that can be achieved quantitatively—the one based on the assumption that Pact M day and NATO M day coincide. Suffice it to say that achievement of this requirement would increase the ability to deter or successfully counter any head start the Pact had in mobilizing, but certainly qualitative improvements should continue to be sought which, when combined with some quantitative increases during mobilization, would assure success.

Based on the previously developed requirements for U.S. divisions in

NATO, given *coincident* NATO and Pact M days, a description of how these requirements can be met is appropriate.

M day: Six divisions of two brigades each. On M day, six U.S. divisions, consisting of two brigades each, would be in place in NATO Center. The third brigade of each division and supporting units would be "dual based"; that is, it would be located in the continental United States (CONUS) but would be airliftable to its parent division and prepositioned equipment in Europe by M + 7. Thus a total of twelve brigades, equivalent to approximately four full divisions, represent the postulated M-day requirement. (It should be noted that this force is about one maneuver brigade less than that currently stationed in Europe.) The mission of the six reduced divisions in Europe and their remaining brigades in CONUS dictates that all these units be fully ready on M day.

M + 7: Six full divisions. On M + 7, the requirement for six full divisions in place would be met by airlifting the third brigade of each of the six divisions to Europe within seven days. This is possible if the necessary equipment for the six brigades and supporting units is prepositioned in Europe, thus requiring the transatlantic transportation of only personnel and baggage. The brigades must also be ready for deployment by M day. Prepositioned equipment could be secured and maintained by the parent division in its area of operation, and airlifted brigades would join their equipment in their assigned areas to assure rapid combat readiness of the full divisions.

M + 15: Seven divisions. By M + 15, another division could be airlifted to join the six already in place. This division also would be "dual based," with its equipment prepositioned in Europe. Since only personnel and baggage would be airlifted, the move should be completed easily within a week.[3] Thus the division could have a readiness objective of M + 7 and still be prepared to move overseas in time to achieve the objective of having seven divisions in Europe by M + 15.

M + 30: Eleven divisions. The requirement of eleven divisions by M + 30 makes this the most severe phase of deployment for the United States. It can be met by adding one Marine and three Army divisions to

3. "According to an official assessment, the Military Airlift Command, with the C-141 *Starlifter* in the passenger role and the C-5A in the freight role, will at this stage [by 1973] be able to move 'an Army division with equipment and six fighter squadrons with support units to Europe in less than one week.' " Trevor Cliffe, *Military Technology and the European Balance,* Adelphi Papers, 89 (London: International Institute for Strategic Studies, 1972), p. 28.

the seven divisions in place by M + 15. The Marine division would move on its own ships from the East Coast to NATO Center within thirty days. To assure this capability, its readiness objective would have to be M day. Of the three Army divisions added, two would move by air and one by sea. If the two airlifted divisions were ready for deployment by M + 7, their men and equipment, according to official estimates, could be moved to Europe within the following three weeks. The mode of transportation for both divisions, given the absence of prepositioned equipment for them in Europe, requires that they be light formations, either infantry or airmobile divisions. The Army division to be moved by ships must be ready on M day and should be an armored or mechanized division since large amounts of heavy, bulky unit equipment can be moved readily only in this way.[4] This division and the Marine division would be the first to require the use of troop convoys to Europe after M day; thus maximum naval protection should be concentrated on these convoys to assure their safe passage, even though D day may not be expected until later.

M + 60: Thirteen divisions. Two more divisions would be necessary in Europe between M + 30 and M + 60. This requirement could be met if two Army divisions, with a readiness objective of M + 30, deployed to Europe by sea convoy at about the same time.

M + 90: Fourteen divisions. By M + 90, another division (for a total of fourteen) is believed necessary, and could be obtained either by fully mobilizing the Marine Reserve division by M + 60 or by using the active Marine division stationed on the West Coast. Enough shipping should be available to transport the division to the Center by M + 90.

M + 120: Eighteen divisions. The M + 120 requirement is eighteen divisions, four more than for M + 90. This could be met by mobilizing four Army National Guard divisions with a readiness objective of M + 90. All four could be transported simultaneously by sea convoy and arrive in the Center by M + 120.

Table C-2 summarizes all U.S. division requirements in NATO Center. The time when each division must achieve combat-ready status is also shown, introducing the concept of the "degrees of readiness" re-

4. Interviews with Department of the Navy sources indicate that, with sufficient troop and cargo ship capability (probably twenty to twenty-five ships for each division), Army divisions could be deployed to Europe from the East or Gulf Coast in twenty to twenty-three days (including loading and unloading), depending on the degree of evasive convoy action required on the open sea.

Table C-2. Summary of U.S. Division Dispositions to Meet NATO Center Requirement

Number and type of force component	*Time at which required in NATO Center*	*Location and disposition*	*Readiness objective*	*Division category*
3 armored divisions at ⅔ strength (minus 1 brigade each)	M day	NATO Central Region (each division secures prepositioned equipment for its brigade based in continental U.S.)	M day	A
3 mechanized divisions at ⅔ strength (minus 1 brigade each)	M day	NATO Central Region (each division secures prepositioned equipment for its brigade based in continental U.S.)	M day	A
3 armored brigades	M + 7	Continental U.S. (airlifted to join parent divisions in NATO Center)	M day	A
3 mechanized brigades	M + 7	Continental U.S. (airlifted to join parent divisions in NATO Center)	M day	A
1 armored division	M + 15	Continental U.S. (airlifted to prepositioned set of equipment in NATO Center)	M + 7	B
1 infantry division	M + 30	Continental U.S. (airlifted with equipment to NATO Center)	M + 7	B
1 airmobile division	M + 30	Continental U.S. (airlifted with equipment to NATO Center)	M + 7	B
1 mechanized division	M + 30	Continental U.S. (moved with equipment to NATO Center by convoy)	M day	A
1 Marine division	M + 30	Continental U.S., East Coast (moved with equipment to NATO Center by amphibious shipping)	M day	A
1 armored division	M + 60	Continental U.S. (moved with equipment to NATO Center by convoy)	M + 30	C
1 mechanized division	M + 60	Continental U.S. (moved with equipment to NATO Center by convoy)	M + 30	C
1 Marine division	M + 90	Continental U.S. (may be Marine Reserve division or West Coast active division moved with equipment to NATO Center by amphibious shipping)	M + 60	D
2 armored divisions (Reserve components)	M + 120	Continental U.S. (National Guard divisions; moved with equipment to NATO Center by convoy)	M + 90	D
2 mechanized divisions[a] (Reserve components)	M + 120	Continental U.S. (National Guard divisions; moved with equipment to NATO Center by convoy)	M + 90	D

a. The current National Guard division posture contains two armored and only one mechanized division. Another mechanized division would have to be formed from existing units; otherwise, one mechanized and one infantry division would be deployed in lieu of two mechanized divisions.

quired for each division. The above discussion has explicitly defined the readiness requirements (or readiness objectives) for all reinforcing divisions. Not all divisions are needed on M day, and to sustain a required buildup over time, divisions need only be ready in time to fulfill their commitment in the Center. Thus one can designate M-day divisions, M + 7 divisions, M + 30 divisions, and so on. In Table C-2 these divisions have been given category designations according to their readiness objectives.[5]

5. A readiness objective of M day is designated category A; an objective of M + 7, category B; an objective of M + 30, category C; and a readiness objective of M + 90 is designated category D (except for the Marine Corps category D division, which has M + 60 readiness).

Table C-3. Current and Proposed Worldwide U.S. Ground Force Posture

Service and disposition	*Current forces*	*Proposed forces*	*Proposed date of mobilization*
Active Army			
Deployed in Europe	2 armored divisions	3 armored divisions[a]	M day
	2⅓ mechanized divisions	3 mechanized divisions[a]	M day
Oriented to Europe, based in continental U.S.	2 armored divisions	3 armored brigades[b]	M day
	1⅔ mechanized divisions	3 mechanized brigades[b]	M day
		1 armored division	M + 7
		1 armored division	M + 30
		1 mechanized division	M day
		1 mechanized division	M + 30
		1 infantry division	M + 7
		1 airmobile division	M + 7
Deployed in Asia (Korea)	1 infantry division	...	...
Oriented to Asia, based in continental U.S. and Hawaii	2 infantry divisions	1 infantry division	M + 7
		1 infantry division	M + 30
Strategic Reserve, based in continental U.S.	1 airborne division	1 airborne division	M day
	1 airmobile division		
Army Reserve			
Based in continental U.S.	1 mechanized division	2 mechanized divisions	M + 90
	2 armored divisions	2 armored divisions	M + 90
	5 infantry divisions	2 infantry divisions	M + 90
	4 mechanized brigades	4 mechanized brigades	M + 60
	1 armored brigade	1 armored brigade	M + 60
	18 infantry brigades	5 infantry brigades	M + 60
	1 airborne brigade	1 airborne brigade	M + 60
	155 battalions	60 battalions	M + 45
Active Marine Corps			
Based on U.S. East Coast	1 division	1 division	M day
Based on U.S. West Coast	1 division	1 division	M + 30
Deployed in Asia/Pacific	1 division	1 division	M day
Marine Corps Reserve			
Based in continental U.S.	1 division	1 division	M + 60

a. Each division contains only two brigades.
b. One brigade is assigned to each of the divisions already in Europe, bringing them to full strength.

Up to now the discussion here has focused exclusively on U.S. requirements with respect to European contingencies; however, the United States' plans for contingencies elsewhere in the world and the requirements for NATO postulated above would significantly affect the ability of the United States to respond to extra-European contingencies. It is thus prudent, when comparing the current U.S. force posture for NATO with that suggested in the analysis, to examine briefly worldwide requirements and determine the various forces needed to fulfill those requirements. Table C-3 summarizes both current and proposed worldwide U.S. ground force posture, including that of major reserve components. The proposed new posture stems from the requirements projected above and is based on the concept of mobilization categories.

At present four and one-third Army divisions are deployed in Europe, with another three and two-thirds oriented toward Europe but located in the continental United States. One Army division is also deployed in Korea, and two more, based in Hawaii and the continental United States, are postured for Asian contingencies. The two remaining active Army divisions are located in the United States and can be considered as part of the strategic reserve. All active divisions have an ostensible readiness objective of M day; however, the authorized manning levels of some divisions place them in a decidedly lesser state of readiness. A definitive statement of the relationship between authorized manning levels and readiness objectives is not available except perhaps in classified planning documents. One of three active Marine divisions is also earmarked for NATO; the other two, because of their disposition, are clearly Asia oriented and could be diverted to NATO only after some delay.

Major reserve component combat units include eight Army divisions (National Guard), twenty-one separate brigades, and 155 separate battalions. Of these units, one mechanized and two armored divisions plus about nine separate brigades are clearly earmarked for NATO, with the remainder available for Asian or other contingencies as required. The Marines' single reserve division is not formally earmarked for any specific contingency, although it is probably more oriented to Asia and the Pacific than to any other part of the world.

A new worldwide ground force posture, based in part on the proposed revisions in U.S. requirements for NATO Center, has six reduced-strength Army divisions in Europe. Six brigades are located in the United States for immediate deployment to fill out the Europe-based formations. Six additional CONUS-based active Army divisions are designated to reinforce Europe. The language of the Nixon Doctrine and the present objectives of the military assistance program for South Korea strongly imply that no U.S. Army divisions will in the future be forward-deployed on the Asian mainland. However, two Army divisions will remain oriented toward Asia from bases in Hawaii and the continental United States. Another assumption is that the Army will contribute only one division to the strategic reserve. It is believed that this reduction from the present two divisions so allocated would not incur undue risk. Most conceivable sequences of contingency deployments probably would allow additional divisions to be designated as a strategic reserve; or reserve component divisions after mobilization might also be used as a strategic reserve. The new posture also retains the Marines' one reserve and three active divisions, but the readiness of all active Marine divisions need not be M day. Some relaxation of readiness for Asia-oriented Marine units is considered appropriate in view of the lower U.S. profile in Asia suggested by the Nixon Doctrine.

In contrast to the present force of thirteen divisions, the new force posture calls for an Army of fifteen divisions, eight of M-day readiness, four of M + 7 readiness, and three of M + 30 readiness. Consonant with the primacy of the NATO contingency, the new posture would also have more active armored and mechanized units than the current one. Moreover, Army National Guard divisions have been reduced from eight to six, and the number of separate brigades and battalions of the reserve components has also been cut. To support Division Forces, 11 separate reserve component brigades are deemed sufficient, or about one brigade per two active and reserve divisions. Brigades could serve as corps troops. The 60 separate battalions are a substantial reduction from the present 155 and could serve as unit replacements after M + 45, particularly in NATO contingencies, or they could be used to support divisions. Of the 60, more than half would be maneuver battalions (infantry and armor) and the remainder artillery and other combat support.

No analysis of U.S. Army Division Force requirements for NATO Center would be complete without a discussion of the combat support and logistics units necessary to sustain the proposed divisions. Sustaining units for Marine divisions are provided by "force troops," both ashore and afloat, using U.S. Navy facilities and resources where appropriate. No modification of this support is anticipated. If, however, Marines were subject to prolonged combat far inland in NATO Center (probably under Army Corps control), provisions would have to be made to augment Army supporting units.

Army divisions are supported in the field by combat support and logistics units, of battalion and group size, operating in corps and army areas under Corps and Field Army Support Command control. For combat support, specialized units provide supporting fire, communications, and engineering assistance. Logistics units provide the division with the necessary supply, medical, personnel, and transportation support to assure sustained operations beyond the capability of organic division support. For planning purposes, combat support and logistics units, which are not organic to divisions but are necessary to support them in the field, are organized into Initial Supporting Increments

(ISI) and Sustaining Supporting Increments (SSI). Each Army Division Force therefore contains one division, one ISI, and one SSI.[6] The ISI consists of supporting units that should be deployed with the division or shortly thereafter and that have the capability of providing supply, transportation, medical, personnel, and combat support to the division for about sixty days. The SSI consists of supporting units similar to those in the ISI, and must be deployed within about sixty days in order to assure sustaining support to the division. The function of the ISI makes it necessary that its units have readiness objectives that are consonant with the division it supports. SSI requirements follow division deployments by a long enough time to permit most SSI units to be located in the reserves.

Table C-4 shows the current ISI and SSI structure in U.S. Army Division Forces. Of the divisions deployed overseas (four and one-third in Europe and one in South Korea), each has an ISI. The two and one-third SSIs stationed in Europe are for the long-term support of U.S. Army forces in NATO. Divisions stationed in the United States and not scheduled for immediate deployment are deemed to have no need of active force ISIs if their readiness objectives will allow the units forming the ISIs to come from mobilized reserves. Thus units of three ISIs that support active divisions are in the reserves. Only one and two-thirds active force SSIs are stationed in the United States. Units making up these SSIs are available for either European or Asian contingencies. Most of the units in SSIs that support active divisions can be located in the reserves since the increments normally should not be needed for at least the first sixty days of division commitment. At present, four SSIs are in the active forces structure, primarily to provide a sustaining support base in Europe in peacetime that can be rapidly expanded for an extended conflict and to provide a flexible support force in the United States for protracted contingencies elsewhere in the world.

The proposed active force posture, based on the postulated U.S. requirements for NATO Center and on assumptions about other requirements worldwide (see Table C-3), contains eight divisions that must have an M-day readiness (Category A), four divisions with a readiness

6. An Army Division Force includes the division and its slice of all support units required within a theater to conduct combat operations. The Division Force consists of three increments: division, ISI, and SSI. The division is an operational organization, while the ISI and SSI are planning concepts only. The planning strength of each increment is sixteen thousand men, thus giving the Division Force a total strength of forty-eight thousand.

Table C-4. Requirements for U.S. Army Supporting Increments, Current and Proposed Posture

Location or readiness objective	*Divisions*	*Initial supporting increments*	*Sustaining supporting increments*
Current			
Active Army			
Deployed	5⅓	5⅓	2⅓
Stationed in U.S.	7⅔	4⅔	1⅔
Total active	13	10	4
Army Reserve components			
Stationed in U.S.	8	11	16⅔
Proposed			
Active Army			
Category A (M day)	8	8	1
Category B (M + 7)	4	4	1
Category C (M + 30)	3	0	0
Total active	15	12	2
Army Reserve components			
Category D (M + 90)	6	9	19

objective of M + 7 (Category B), and three divisions ready by M + 30 (Category C). Only the Category A and B divisions need ISIs in the active structure since Category C divisions, which need not be ready for deployment until M + 30, can draw their ISIs from reserve forces.[7] Only two SSIs would be in the active forces. One would be a Category A SSI deployed in Europe to support units stationed there. This is a reduction of one and one-third SSIs now in Europe and is in consonance with the presumption of a short conflict there and the need for an increased combat-to-support ratio in that theater. The other active SSI, whose units would have M + 7 readiness, would be stationed in the United States as a flexible force for worldwide deployment. They would provide a capability for early establishment of a theater support network that would permit sustained operations of divisions that might be deployed into the theater. Reserve components are postulated to contain six National Guard divisions, the ISIs and SSIs for those divisions, and additional ISIs (three) and SSIs (thirteen) to round out the active division force structure when needed.

The above analysis acknowledges the primacy of Europe in U.S. strategic planning. However, as was noted earlier, contingencies else-

7. The size and type of units from the reserves that make up an ISI are such that they should achieve readiness in thirty days or less after being called to active duty.

where could occur, and, depending on the sequence of events, forces for NATO could be a major factor in the response to the non-NATO contingencies. Thus to compare and evaluate current and proposed ground force postures for NATO, it is appropriate to examine the total force requirement. For NATO, the requirement has been developed in detail; for other contingencies, marginal adjustments based on the current posture for Asia and the need for a strategic reserve have been made. Though somewhat cursory in nature for areas outside NATO, this rationale does allow a reasonable comparison of current and proposed NATO land forces within a total land forces structure. Manpower and cost differences can be readily discerned.

APPENDIX D

Opposing Force Dispositions in Central Europe

Table D-1 shows the current disposition of NATO and Warsaw Pact ground forces in the Central Region and their potential for augmentation.[1] Allied Forces Central Region (AFCENT) contains two Army groups: Northern Army Group (NORTHAG) and Central Army Group (CENTAG). Each has four Army corps made up of national forces aligned along the East-West border. Only the French First Army's two divisions deployed in West Germany and Canada's one-third division equivalent are not on line. Opposing NATO in the Central Region are Warsaw Pact divisions from East Germany, Poland, Czechoslovakia, and the Soviet Union.

Previous analysis has evaluated forces in the Central Region in the aggregate without regard to their tactical deployment; but Table D-1 shows the Pact currently disposed according to a tactical plan that heavily weights an axis of attack in the north. In sharp contrast are NATO deployments, which favor the central and southern sectors of the Central Region. Thus although the Pact initially musters a less than 2:1 ground advantage in the Central Region as a whole, the balance of forces in the north is decidedly unfavorable to NATO. For example, NATO divisions in the northern sector are now outnumbered 2:1 by Pact divisions; by M + 30, the Pact obtains a nearly 3:1 advantage, a margin of superiority which increases to almost 3.4:1 by M + 120.

The assumed Warsaw Pact strategy is one that places the major emphasis in the north against NORTHAG—more specifically, across the North German Plain. One-half of East Germany's divisions, the majority of Polish forces, and about 55 percent of the Soviet divisions are as-

1. The division is used as the unit of measurement to simplify calculations and because, although Pact divisions are smaller than NATO divisions, they are roughly comparable in numbers of tanks and combat troops.

Table D-1. Current and Proposed NATO Division Disposition in the Central Region Opposing Warsaw Pact Divisions, and Their Projected Augmentation, M Day to M + 120

NATO

Group, country, or requirement	Current disposition of divisions[a]							Proposed disposition of divisions[b]						
	M day	*M + 7*	*M + 15*	*M + 30*	*M + 60*	*M + 90*	*M + 120*	*M day*	*M + 7*	*M + 15*	*M + 30*	*M + 60*	*M + 90*	*M + 120*
Northern Army Group														
Netherlands	2	2	2	3	3	3	3	2	2	2	3	3	3	3
West Germany	4	5	5	5	5	5	5	4	6	6	6	6	6	6
United Kingdom	3	3	3	4	5	5	5	3	3	3	4	5	5	5
Belgium	2	2	2	3	3	3	3	2	2	2	3	3	3	3
United States	...	...	...	...	...	...	...	2	3	4	6	8	8	11
Total	11	12	12	15	16	16	16	13	16	17	22	25	25	28
Divisions required[d]	11	16	17	22	25	25	27	11	16	17	22	25	25	27
Surplus or shortage	0	−4	−5	−7	−9	−9	−11	+2	0	0	0	0	0	+1
Central Army Group (*northern sector*)														
West Germany	4	5	5	5	5	5	5	4	5	5	5	5	5	5
Canada	⅓	⅓	⅓	1	1	1	1	⅓	⅓	⅓	1	1	1	1
France	...	...	...	...	...	...	...	...	2	2	2	4	4	4
United States	2	3	4	8	10	10	11	2	3	3	5	5	6	7
Total	6⅓	8⅓	9⅓	14	16	16	17	6⅓	10⅓	10⅓	13	15	16	17
Divisions required[d]	7	10	10	13	16	16	17	7	10	10	13	16	16	17
Surplus or shortage	−⅔	−1⅔	−⅔	+1	0	0	0	−⅔	+⅓	+⅓	0	−1	0	0
Central Army Group (*southern sector*)														
West Germany	3	4	4	4	4	4	4	3	3	3	3	3	3	3
France	2	5	5	7	10	10	10	2	3	3	5	6	6	6
United States	2	3	3	3	3	4	7	...	...	...	...	...	...	...
Total	7	12	12	14	17	18	21	5	6	6	8	9	9	9
Divisions required[d]	6	6	7	9	9	9	9	6	6	7	9	9	9	9
Surplus or shortage	+1	+6	+5	+5	+8	+9	+12	−1	0	−1	−1	0	0	0

Warsaw Pact[c]

Axis of attack or country	*M day*	*M + 7*	*M + 15*	*M + 30*	*M + 60*	*M + 90*	*M + 120*
Major axis (*North German Plain*)							
East Germany	3	3	3	3	3	3	3
Poland	2	10	10	10	10	10	10
Soviet Union	15	17	20	30	37	37	41
Total	20	30	33	43	50	50	54
Minor axis (*Fulda Gap*)							
East Germany	3	3	3	3	3	3	3
Poland	...	3	3	3	3	3	3
Soviet Union	10	12	14	20	25	25	27
Total	13	18	20	26	31	31	33
Secondary zone (*south*)							
Czechoslovakia	10	10	10	12	12	12	12
Soviet Union	2	2	3	5	5	5	6
Total	12	12	13	17	17	17	18

a. For non-U.S. NATO countries, NATO buildups use national command forces as postulated in Table A-1 (Case II). Nations on line deploy forces to current corps areas. The French and the Canadians are considered deployed near their current locations. For U.S. deployments, divisions are allocated to current U.S. corps dispositions with more weight to northern corps.

b. For non-U.S. NATO countries, NATO buildups use national command forces as postulated in Table A-1 (Case II). Nations on line deploy forces to corps areas shown. Canadians are deployed in vicinity of current location near the center. French forces are initially deployed in southern sector; some French reinforcements are postulated for deployment to the central sector. For U.S. deployments, it is recommended that one corps be deployed to the Northern Army Group (NORTHAG) and reinforced with greatest weight. The West German corps in NORTHAG gets an additional division.

c. Disposition shown postulates tactical plan to conduct major attack in the north (North German Plain) with minor attack in the center (Fulda Gap–Frankfurt axis) and economy-of-force operations in the secondary zone (along the Czech border). Consequently about 55 percent of Soviet divisions are disposed in the north, 35 to 40 percent in the center, and 5–10 percent in the south.

d. NATO divisions required are based on the definitions of Condition 2 for M day and M + 7 and on Condition 3 for M + 15 to M + 120, which were described in Appendix C. U.S. divisions deployed are based on assessed requirements in Appendix C.

sumed to be employed along this front. Another likely invasion corridor, although narrower, is the "minor axis" through the Fulda Gap directed at the Frankfurt area. An attack there would encounter the one West German and the one U.S. corps currently in the northern sector of CENTAG. Pact forces available for combat in the area consist of the remaining East German divisions, a few Polish forces, and about 35 to 40 percent of the Soviet divisions deployed in the Central Region. The south is considered to be a secondary zone of operations for the Pact; Pact forces there consist of enough divisions disposed along the Czechoslovakian-West German border to fix opposing NATO forces in place and to conduct economy-of-force operations, taking advantage of whatever opportunities present themselves. All Czech and 5 to 10 percent of Soviet divisions are believed to be deployable here.

NATO deployments in Table D-1 represent those postulated under Case II (see Appendix Table A-1) for non-U.S. NATO forces and the posture developed in Appendix C for the American forces. (U.S. dispositions are split between their two corps, with heavier emphasis on the more threatened northern corps.) National zones remain intact and post–M-day deployments of non-U.S. NATO forces are to their respective national zones. French and Canadian formations, while not currently on line, are assumed to be deployed near their present locations. Dutch, West German, British, and Belgian forces are deployed in NORTHAG. Reinforcements to NORTHAG from national commands operating in CENTAG are not expected and in fact would be difficult to plan for because of the lack of tactical flexibility in the current command and control, organizational, and logistics structure of NATO forces. The NATO divisions required in the north are described, given the presumption of a major threat there. The requirement is based on Condition 2 in Table C-1 for M day and M + 7.[2] From M + 15 to M + 120, the NATO division requirement is based on Condition 3.[3]

The obvious result of present NATO force dispositions and plans, which call for allied reinforcement of their respective corps, is to place in serious jeopardy the ability of the Atlantic Alliance to defend NATO Center successfully without resort to nuclear weapons. Both on M day

2. NATO divisions do not allow the Pact to achieve more than a 1.5:1 division advantage, and NATO divisions are assumed to be qualitatively 25 percent better than Pact divisions.

3. NATO divisions do not allow the Pact to achieve a better than 2:1 division advantage, and opposing divisions are considered qualitatively equal (1:1).

and beyond, along key sectors of the Central Front, NATO fails to maintain vis-à-vis the Pact the ratio of forces deemed necessary to halt and contain an attack. For example, astride the most likely avenue of invasion (the North German Plain) as mobilization proceeds, NATO suffers an ever-increasing shortfall, which reaches ominous proportions as early as M + 7. Conversely, in the southern sector, the least likely target of a major Pact thrust, the United States, France, and West Germany maintain substantially more forces than appear necessary to meet the threat in that sector. And if, as some strategists have suggested, the Fulda Gap is the most threatened area, a Pact buildup there, at the expense of its forces in the North German Plain, would still result in the same serious imbalance since large NATO forces in the south would probably remain in position, engaging a smaller Pact force in that area.

Table D-1 also shows the authors' proposed redisposition of NATO forces to meet the requirements discussed above. All "M-day" NATO forces (except for the French and the Canadians) are positioned on line and are better disposed to counter aggression in the Central Region's northern sector. Pursuant to that goal the southernmost U.S. corps has been transferred from CENTAG to NORTHAG and placed on line between the British and Belgian corps. Post–M-day modifications in deployments include: (1) the heavy reinforcement of the U.S. corps in NORTHAG relative to that of the U.S. corps in CENTAG; (2) the transfer of a division from the West German corps in the south to the German corps in NORTHAG; and (3) the deployment of enough incoming French divisions to the Fulda Gap area to assure a desirable balance there. Large French forces would be retained in the southern sector to cover the secondary threat.

From this repositioning of forces emerges a defense of the Central Region that is tactically and geographically much more attuned to the real threat than is currently the case. In NORTHAG, NATO has the forces needed to halt and contain a Pact attack there. At M day they are particularly strong (about two divisions more than the required number). In the Fulda Gap area NATO forces also meet requirements except on M day and M + 60. The M-day shortfall is minor, however, and in that sector overall NATO forces should be enough to contain aggression. In the South, NATO forces would be weaker than at present as a result of the transfer of divisions northward to the more threatened areas. However, NATO could conduct economy-of-force operations in the South and, if necessary, give some ground to gain time. Since the terrain in that sector strongly favors the defender, a slight shortfall in NATO divisions there would not be critical.

If the Fulda Gap should be the primary focus of a Pact buildup, the proposed posture would be flexible enough to respond to such a tactic. The destination of some U.S. reinforcements could be changed from NORTHAG to CENTAG after M day, and one or two West German divisions in the North could also be redeployed southward.